Emotional Intelligence for the Modern Workplace

A Guide to Developing Emotional Intelligence and Ensuring Psychological Safety

Morten Johnson

Table of Contents

Introduction

The business world has been under pressure since the outbreak of the COVID-19 pandemic in 2020, and geopolitical tension and its economic consequences have been making for a greater impact on companies and their employees since then. Life has become more stressful for most people across the globe, and there is still no end in sight to the situation.

Emotionally intelligent leadership is becoming increasingly important during these challenging times, and businesses that employ managers with these qualities stand a much better chance of surviving and growing in the current economic climate.

For a business to succeed on every level, you need leaders who will understand their emotions, as well as those of other people. In recent years, it has become clear that high emotional intelligence (EQ) is a vital requirement for good leaders, as they can use their good interpersonal and communication skills to their advantage. These managers are also good at retaining talented staff and reducing staff turnover.

This book will consider how sufficient emotional intelligence (EQ) can help organizations create an atmosphere of psychological safety for their teams. What causes a lack of psychological safety in companies and how can this be overcome? How can psychological safety benefit your company and help your employees have more fulfilling careers?

In the post-COVID world, it's going to be the companies that offer their employees the opportunity to speak their minds freely, without having to fear retribution, that will attract the most talented employees. For many people, it's simply not an option any longer to work for companies where management rules their teams through fear. Who wants to work for a company where you can lose your job when you voice your opinion? Employees also can't make valuable contributions to the company if they feel they will be censured when they give input.

Instead of making employees fear failure, companies should have a process whereby they document what can be learned from failures and mistakes at work. Employees should be encouraged to learn from each other, and not mock one another when they make mistakes at work.

This book also focuses on the fact that companies should encourage emotional understanding and self-awareness among their employees, to help teams build emotional connections and have empathy for each other. Your company will be more productive, and it will add to your bottom line if your staff members are able to interact with each other in a mature and understanding way.

The main difference between high-functioning teams and low-functioning ones is psychological safety. Teams fare well when all the members feel confident enough to speak up. To be able to get to this place, and establish psychological safety, managers and leaders in an organization will have to model boundaries that can't be crossed. Employees need to understand how their behavior contributes to psychological safety and they need to be empowered with the emotional skills to create it for themselves and everyone around them.

Presentations alone won't have the desired effect when it comes to establishing psychological safety. Managers need to live the values of the company and model the respectful behavior they want other employees to follow, by treating everyone with respect. As a manager, you need to call out disrespectful behavior when you observe it, for example, if employees shoot down each other's ideas during meetings. This might feel awkward at the beginning but it can encourage real change in the company.

No one wants to be ridiculed at work, and team members need to be encouraged to show an interest in each other's contributions.

Advocating their own ideas, but showing an interest in the ideas of others, will allow idea generation to flourish in your organization.

In our violent society, emotional intelligence can also play an important role in minimizing volatility in the workplace. Employees who manage to stay cool in difficult situations will be more rational, which will lead to better results for the company and a safer work environment.

Improving Emotional Intelligence as a Leader

As a leader, you will first need to consider your own level of emotional intelligence and how it can be improved before you can create a psychologically safe environment for your company. You can only start to make changes once you're able to recognize what is responsible for your thoughts, feelings, and behavior.

It's essential that everyone in the organization should understand how their emotions and behavior affect the people around them. Even if you hadn't learned all the emotional intelligence skills you needed to in childhood, it's still possible to improve your emotional intelligence skills as an adult.

All employees need to be able to manage their emotions, as they will be able to build better relationships at work, which will lead to improved productivity.

Preventing Burnout

Burnout is becoming increasingly prevalent in businesses across the globe, and managers are especially at risk to become victims of this soul-destroying condition. An essential management skill is the ability to delegate successfully, which also reduces stress levels. As a manager, you need to stop doing so much of the technical work yourself, and assign some of the responsibilities to your staff, which will also provide them with growth opportunities.

If you can see multiple reasons not to delegate, you need to change your mindset. Your employees need a chance to learn, otherwise, you will continue to be overwhelmed.

Delegating will also build the trust between you and your staff, and they will become more engaged with their work, which will improve your company's staff retention.

Habits to Help You Relieve Stress

This book also considers habits that can help you manage your stress levels. Managers experience more stress, and a lot more is expected from them, when it comes to accountability. It's essential to learn to identify your triggers and determine the main causes for your feelings. Mindful meditation is a useful activity when it comes to stress relief.

Mindfulness helps you focus on the work you are doing now, in the present. This is becoming an even more useful and essential skill in the daily overload we experience at work as part of the knowledge economy. It has many benefits for the workplace and can also increase emotional intelligence.

Mindfulness can give you the inner reserve of calm you need to cope with a stressful career while still being productive. It can also help you be more creative and help you focus better. You will face many distractions during your workday and mindfulness can help you improve your ability to concentrate.

If you want to implement mindfulness in your team, it needs to be voluntary. Employees should never be pressured to take part in it, as it's just one of the tools that can promote employee wellness. The aim of mindfulness is not to increase productivity, but you may find that productivity will increase as a by-product.

Time to Reflect

Business leaders need to reflect on their successes and failures every day. It's vital that you set aside 20 to 30 minutes to think about what worked well in your team and what didn't. Where were your employees successful and where could they have done better? What were your emotions when things didn't go according to plan, and how was your performance as a leader affected?

Daily self-reflection will help you learn and improve because you need to see things as they really are, and not only forever in a positive light. Being honest when you reflect will help you make better decisions.

Getting to Know Each Other

You need to become invested in creating a psychologically safe work environment, and get to know your employees and what gets them through their days. Showing an interest in your employees will also build trust between you and them. You need to show your employees that you value them more than simply workers and that you care about them as people.

You might find this difficult, but it's a good idea to ask your employees for feedback on your performance. Different people will experience you in different ways, and you can learn a lot from their feedback.

Practicing Empathy

We spend a lot of time at work, and it's extremely difficult to go to work in a toxic work environment where the office is hostile and unfriendly. Empathy will assist management to facilitate a supportive office culture where rapport can be built between management, coworkers, and clients.

Empathy can also help build authentic relationships with customers and clients if the environment of the company is customer-centric.

The book also asks you to consider how your employees' current behavior could be influenced by unresolved issues from childhood. People often suffer the emotional consequences of unresolved childhood trauma in adulthood. Repressed childhood feelings could cause people to attempt to dominate and abuse others around them. Denial of childhood pain makes it almost impossible for many people to experience empathy as adults.

Effective Feedback

The book also considers how managers can give effective feedback.

Being able to give respectful feedback to employees, as well as creating an open culture of sharing thoughts and knowledge are also essential aspects of creating a psychologically safe work environment. Managers need to be able to give behavior-specific feedback consistently and regularly. Employees shouldn't be surprised by the feedback they receive during formal performance appraisals.

Creating an atmosphere of trust is also part of creating psychological safety in your organization. Management should have an open-door policy (with limits) and employees should feel free to ask for the information they need. Requests for information should be viewed as opportunities for education and to create connections between people.

Conflict Management

Experiencing conflict in your team is a normal part of day-to-day life. If conflict isn't managed properly, it can become an ongoing problem and cause rifts between people and destroy relationships. Disagreements are inevitable when people are from different backgrounds and have different views and opinions.

Conflict can lead to the blame game, which is always an unnecessary waste of time in a busy workplace. One of the ways to prevent this from happening, is to get to know your team members as well as possible. The more they know about each other's different ways of viewing the world, the less likely conflict and personality clashes are likely to occur. Personality tests are also useful in determining the strengths of your team members.

Core Message

The core message of this book is that it's the responsibility of management to create a psychologically safe work environment for employees.

However, before you can do this, you need to focus on the development of your own emotional intelligence. Before you can change the culture of your company, ask yourself if you are an emotionally healthy person. Are you fully equipped to deal with the stress and challenges that come your way? If you are struggling, it's time that you need to start looking where you have to make changes and if you need help to do so.

I want to invite you to use this book as a guide on your journey not only to increasing your own emotional intelligence, but also that of your employees. Together, you can create a psychologically safe work environment.

Chapter 1:

What Is Emotional Intelligence?

Emotional intelligence, namely being able to identify and manage emotions, as well as build stable relationships, is becoming increasingly important in the world today, especially in our ever-changing knowledge economy.

Leaders, employees, and entrepreneurs all need emotional intelligence to thrive in their businesses and careers. Companies that want to achieve their business goals and remain successful are going to have to move away from toxic work environments and create effective environments where people feel safe and have enough confidence to share their thoughts, ideas, and even emotions with their colleagues and managers. In our modern business environment, we need organizations that are characterized by emotional intelligence, not only in the way that leaders and employees interact with each other but also in how they treat customers.

It's becoming increasingly evident that to lead a successful, productive, and happy life, you will need both emotional intelligence (EI) and a high emotional quotient (EQ). A high intelligence quotient (IQ) by itself is no longer sufficient to ensure success in work and life.

Emotional Intelligence (EI), Emotional Quotient (EQ), and Intelligence Quotient (IQ)

Emotional Intelligence (EI)

Emotionally intelligent people are able to identify and manage their emotions. You should also be able to recognize the emotions of other people and treat them with empathy. This ability enables you to communicate effectively and will assist you to build and sustain healthy relationships with others.

As mentioned in the Introduction, if you hadn't learned emotional intelligence skills as a child, you can learn emotional intelligence in adulthood and improve these valuable skills throughout your life.

Emotional Quotient (EQ)

EQ measures a person's ability to be aware of their emotions, how they cope with pressure and the demands of life, if they are able to control their thoughts, and the actions which are the result of these actions. This measurement tool is supposed to be similar to the IQ measurement, but its validity has been questioned, as there is not a standard of measurement, as there is for IQ.

Intelligence Quotient (IQ)

IQ measures a person's ability to solve problems, and to reason. This is based on how well you fare on certain tests, compared to other people in your age group. IQ can predict academic success, but not success in life. Many people with high IQs don't do well in life, while some people with average IQs end up being super successful.

What Are Emotions?

All of us experience a wide range of emotions every day. Everyone has felt angry, shy, happy, and scared at some stage. We behave according to the emotions we feel, and they can also influence our decision-making.

Where Are Emotions Processed in the Brain?

The hypothalamus, amygdala, hippocampus, and limbic cortex play an important role in the processing of emotions.

The amygdala prepares your body to deal with emotions like fear and anger, by triggering certain emotional responses. The body's fight-or-flight response can be triggered, which prepares you to flee to safety, if you are in danger, or to stay and face it.

If the amygdala were to be removed from your brain, you wouldn't be able to understand the emotional significance of events. Your life would be less meaningful without this ability, and it's likely that you will lose interest in other people. Without your amygdala, you won't be able to recognize feelings.

It seems the amygdala is responsible for all passion, as animals that had their amygdalas removed were found to not feel fear or become angry. These animals lose the urge to cooperate or compete, and they no longer have a place in their species' social order.

Why Do We Need Emotions?

Emotions motivate us to take action. For example, if you really want that promotion at work, you are going to need to work hard to get it.

You will usually take action to ensure that you experience more positive emotions than negative ones. We tend to put ourselves in situations where we can experience excitement and happiness, or at least contentment. We tend to avoid situations that make us feel bored, anxious, or sad.

Other emotional reactions can include confronting someone when you are angry or when you become scared, and removing yourself from a potentially dangerous situation.

In a nutshell, when it comes to decision-making, emotions help us act quickly to ensure that we are successful at what we want to achieve, or that we can survive dangerous situations.

Emotions also assist us to communicate with other people. Communication between people involves cues so that they can understand how the different parties are feeling. This includes body language and facial expressions, as well as verbal information. For example, happy people will be relaxed, smile, and have open body language. While your body language provides information to other people about your state of mind, you'll also be able to get the same information from their body language.

Your emotions also help you process the environment in which you find yourself. They help you understand situations, and signal to you that you may need to respond to something.

It's never a good idea to suppress or ignore your emotions, as they are there to guide, teach, and ultimately protect you.

Core Emotions

The core emotions are also known as root or primary emotions. All other emotions are based on these deeper emotions, and if you understand them, you will be better able to manage the secondary emotions that influence your behavior.

We are capable of mixing emotions and feeling them at different intensities.

No emotion can be regarded as better or worse, and there is no right or wrong way to feel. Every emotion you feel is valuable, as it teaches you something about yourself.

The emotions that have been identified as core emotions are happiness, anger, fear, disgust, surprise, interest, sadness, and shame.

- Anger is the most powerful core emotion that you can feel, and it's difficult to control it. The emotion can be described as an intense feeling of displeasure and hostility. You can experience different layers of anger; anything from being slightly annoyed to becoming enraged. Uncontrolled anger can damage your relationships and cause problems for you at work, as well as in your personal life. Anger can be used in a constructive way, for example, when we are unhappy at work because we don't get along with our boss, we can use our anger to motivate us to look for a new job.

- Fear is essential for our survival, and we usually feel it when we perceive something as being a threat. Your senses will be sharper and you will feel your heart rate increase when you feel fear. It's important to keep your fear under control, as it may have negative effects on your physical health.

- Happiness is a feeling of well-being and joy. This emotion is good for your physical health.

- Surprise can be positive or negative, and can also trigger your flight or fight response. You will usually remember events that caused you to feel this way.

- Everyone experiences sadness or grief, but it can become depression if you feel it too often. The intensity of sadness will be different for different people.

- The core emotion of disgust develops to help people determine what food is safe to eat. We feel it as revulsion.

- Interest makes us want to know something more about a topic or event. This emotion motivates us to enrich our lives.
- You can feel shame for something you've done, or for what you perceive to be your shortcomings. You should try to deal with shame in a healthy way, as it can affect your emotional and physical wellbeing.

The Five Components of EI

There are five components of emotional intelligence, namely self-awareness, self-management, social awareness, empathy, and motivation.

Self-Awareness

Self-awareness is vital for emotional intelligence. Besides recognizing your emotions, you also need to be aware of the effect your emotions, moods, and actions have on other people.

If you want to improve your self-awareness, you need to be able to monitor your emotions, recognize how you react emotionally to different events and situations, and also be able to identify each emotion. If you are self-aware, you will be able to see why your emotions are making you behave in a certain way.

Self-aware people are also able to recognize their own strengths and weaknesses. They are open to feedback and new experiences, and capable of learning from interacting with other people. They are also confident and aware of how other people see them.

There are ways you can improve your self-awareness:

- Pay attention to your thoughts and feelings.

- Think about your experiences.
- Make sure your self-talk is positive, and practice being mindful.
- Set goals for yourself and pursue your passions in life.
- Learn new skills and ask for constructive feedback.
- Establish a growth mindset.

Self-Management

Regulating and managing your own emotions means you can wait for the right time and place to express your feelings. If you can self-regulate, you are able to express your emotions appropriately.

People who excel at self-management are usually flexible and they deal well with change. They can deal with conflict and manage difficult and tense situations. People who are good at self-regulating are also conscientious, and they take responsibility for their actions and how they influence others.

You can improve your self-management in the following ways:

- Pay attention to your thoughts and feelings.
- Find ways to manage stress and difficult situations.
- If you experience challenges, regard them as opportunities.
- Know that you can choose how to respond to someone.
- Accept your emotions and use cognitive reframing to change your emotional responses and thought patterns.
- Work on your communication skills.

Social-Awareness and Handling Relationships

You can improve your emotional awareness by paying attention to the human interactions taking place around you. Pay attention to people's body language, their facial expressions, and what they are saying. This will help you improve your ability to be empathetic.

Being able to interact well with others is also an important part of emotional intelligence. If you are able to build meaningful relationships with others, you can develop a stronger understanding of yourself, and of the other people in your life.

When you understand your own emotions and those of others, you need to be able to use this information in your daily interactions, and in the way you communicate.

This skill is useful in the professional work environment for building relationships between employees and managers, as well as among coworkers. Active listening skills, verbal and nonverbal communication, persuasiveness, and leadership are important social skills.

You can improve your social skills in the following ways:

- Practice active listening and show an interest in others.
- Practice good eye contact and watch your body language.
- Find ways to start conversations with people.

Inspirational leaders also have good relationship management skills and can guide and motivate their staff with their vision. They excel at developing their staff by providing feedback and guidance. Furthermore, they are capable of managing conflict in their teams.

Empathy

The ability to understand how others are feeling is vital to emotional intelligence. However, this is more than just understanding the emotional state of someone you are interacting with; it's also about how you respond to someone based on this information. How would you respond if you sense someone is depressed? Would you treat them more carefully and make an effort to cheer them up?

If you are empathetic, you will also have a better understanding of the power dynamics that affect social relationships, especially in workplaces. It's easier for people with this skill to understand who holds the power in different relationships and situations. They can read the organizational politics and decision networks in a business.

You can improve your empathy by:

- Talking to new people, and sharing your own feelings.
- Listening to people.
- Imagining yourself in another person's situation.
- Engaging in good causes, such as volunteering.

Motivation

Intrinsic motivation is another essential emotional intelligence skill. Emotionally intelligent people are motivated beyond external rewards like fame and money. They have a passion for the field in which they excel, for example writing or acting. They usually set goals for themselves, have a need to achieve, and are both committed and competent at taking the initiative.

You can increase your internal motivation by:

- Setting measurable goals for yourself.
- Setting challenges for yourself to make things interesting, and celebrate your results when you achieve something.

Key Takeaways

- Leaders, employees, and entrepreneurs need emotional intelligence to thrive in their businesses and careers.

- Work environments can be considered psychologically safe when employees feel confident enough to share their thoughts, ideas, and even emotions with their teams.

- Emotionally intelligent people can identify and manage their emotions. They are also able to recognize the emotions of others and treat them with empathy.

- There are five components of emotional intelligence, namely self-awareness, self-management, social awareness, empathy, and motivation.

Chapter 2:

Emotional Intelligence Is Vital for Business Success

According to research that was done in 2009 by Travis Bradberry, the co-author of *Emotional Intelligence 2.0*, EQ has become the strongest predictor of performance in organizations. Up to 90 percent of top performers have high EQs, while people with average IQs outperform those with high IQ most of the time.

Professional employees can develop their EQ by gaining more experience and education, and organizations can identify employees who need to improve their emotional intelligence and develop strategies that will allow them to do so.

The Importance of Psychological Safety in Organizations

The research of psychologist Daniel Goleman and others has shown that emotional intelligence is an essential requirement for good leaders.

Leaders with high EQ will be able to ensure greater team satisfaction and better outcomes for the company in general, as they will be able to use their good interpersonal and communication skills to their advantage.

It's becoming increasingly clear that those companies who are the most successful and attract the most talented employees are those who are able to make their employees feel safe, and offer them the opportunity to speak their minds freely.

We all know the stories of the company where you have to walk on eggshells around management and be really careful about what you say, as you may end up losing your job or being demoted. Have you ever worked for a company where you felt you could make a valuable contribution, but you were too scared to open your mouth to tell them what you thought? It's a terrible feeling when you know you can contribute and make a difference, but you end up being too scared of the potential consequences to open your mouth.

Companies that aim for long-term success will need to make an effort to make their employees feel psychologically safe. Employees should be able to share their perspectives, give input, and make mistakes, all without the constant fear of being punished in some way. No one should fear failure, and the company should instead have a process to document what can be learned from mistakes and failures.

Unfortunately, the cultures of many companies promote an absence of psychological safety, although it might not be that obvious at first. Disempowerment may happen slowly, and employees may lose their confidence or find themselves becoming unsure of themselves, after being with the company for only a short time.

Alphabet, Google's parent company, conducted a study that observed that employees who are protected from criticism are more prepared to take on risky projects.

Employees who are scared to give input won't be able to contribute to the growth and adaptability of the company. When this happens, the company loses the opportunity to make gains from valuable knowledge and talent.

Companies should run projects to encourage self-awareness among their employees, as well as emotional understanding among colleagues, encourage self-management during difficult situations, and an understanding of how to become more productive. Psychological safety also encourages emotional connections and empathy.

The intensive study done by Google on the functioning of teams indicated that the main characteristic that differentiates high-functioning and low-functioning teams is psychological safety. The members of a certain team have to be confident that they won't be embarrassed, or punished for speaking up.

You need courageous leadership to create a psychologically safe organization. Ridiculing and mocking employees in public means they will be less likely to make contributions or admit to mistakes, which other employees could possibly learn from.

To establish psychological safety in the workplace, managers and leaders will have to model the boundaries that can't be crossed. All employees must understand what behaviors create and destroy psychological safety, and they need to have the emotional skills to create that safety.

PowerPoint presentations and training sessions on the company's values often don't have the desired effect. Managers need to live the values and actively model the correct behavior. For example, they can do this by addressing issues where people face put-downs after they made contributions during meetings. This might be awkward for a while, but it sets a standard and new direction for employee behavior.

How You Can Encourage Emotionally Intelligent Behavior

There are ways in which companies can coach people to develop the right behavior that will foster psychological safety in a company.

To be able to contribute to the organization's psychological safety, employees have to understand and think about the characteristics of people who make them feel safe in order to give feedback and provide input on difficult issues without feeling that the person will retaliate or criticize them.

Managers should ask their teams to come up with some rules for not shaming each other. These rules should include not publicly ridiculing each other, especially during staff meetings. Employees should provide each other with constructive feedback on the merits and challenges of an idea. The person who put the idea forward should never be attacked for their contribution.

Teams should be encouraged to show an interest in each other's perspectives and ideas. The strongest organizations encourage their employees to advocate their own ideas, but also show an interest in their colleagues' ideas. Idea generation will flourish in a creative and innovative environment.

If your company has a dysfunctional culture, it's going to take time to educate employees on understanding psychological safety and how it's created.

The research of psychologist Daniel Goleman done in 2002 has shown that emotional intelligence is an essential requirement for good leaders, and companies with emotionally intelligent employees will run better in general.

Emotional intelligence in the workplace starts with empathy, as this allows leaders and managers to understand each other and communicate more effectively, as well as relieve their stress in positive ways.

Emotionally intelligent leaders will make sure all employees feel they are visible and heard by management.

Emotional intelligence can also help minimize emotional volatility in the workplace. Employees who can stay cool in difficult situations will tend to be more rational, which will lead to better results for the company in the long-term. These types of employees are usually also more productive and satisfied with their jobs.

Jane and Lucy's Stories

Jane was an intelligent and talented communications professional. Self-confident and arrogant, she made sure everyone around her was aware of this fact. She enjoyed shooting down other people's ideas and would tell everyone about her Master's Degree in Communications.

After several years as a top performer at her company, Jane got bored. She decided to start her own content agency. Jane's business was successful from the start. Jane made a good impression on everyone who met her. She made big promises to her potential clients on how she would help them grow their businesses through her marketing and social media campaigns. Jane soon signed up many clients and she struggled to recruit employees fast enough to keep up with the work.

Jane's employees at first didn't mind that they were often expected to work late and over weekends. Jane told them that this was for their own benefits, as the business would continue to grow rapidly, which would mean their remuneration would also increase.

After a while, however, they noticed that while the business was indeed growing its client base, their salaries weren't increasing, as Jane had promised. Jane's secretary also received clients from freelancers who hadn't been paid for work that had already been completed and submitted months ago. When she raised this issue, Jane just shrugged it off and didn't respond.

Then, when staff felt that they were already drowning under all the work, Jane informed her employees that they would now have to work late most days. Jane assured them that this arrangement would only be for a limited time. However, her employees didn't trust her any longer, and started looking for other jobs.

Jane ignored any complaints she received and her staff found it increasingly difficult to get hold of her at work. After a while, it became clear that she was doing her best to avoid people.

After a major project went wrong, Jane really started showing her nasty side. She immediately fired the project manager and two other staff members.

She did this at a meeting where all the other employees were present, as she wanted it to be a lesson for them. The culture in the company gradually became even more toxic and people became scared to give input during meetings, and the staff turnover increased exponentially.

Jane lost most of her experienced employees and this affected the work she had to deliver to clients, as the company had a constant influx of new employees who first had to be trained before they could start delivering. New employees were also thrown in at the deep end, and they weren't properly trained or supported before they were expected to take on important work. Many new employees didn't make it through the probation period and ended up leaving the company quickly.

Even when the company made a big loss at the end of the year, Jane refused to acknowledge that she might be partially responsible, and blamed the quality of the work on her remaining employees. Two of her senior managers quit after Jane's outburst at the meeting, leaving her most important department without experienced leadership. The staff turnover started to eat at Jane's company's bottom line, and she also found it increasingly difficult to recruit new staff members, as she had built up a reputation as an abusive employer in her industry. After a tumultuous two years, Jane was forced to close her business.

***

Like Jane, Lucy also started a content agency. However, unlike Jane, she was aware that she didn't know everything in her industry, and that she would have to surround herself with knowledgeable experts if she wanted to succeed.

Lucy decided to only appoint a few experienced and qualified people at first, who would help her grow her company. She treated her managers with respect and listened to their input when it came to appointing employees. Lucy made sure she surrounded herself with people who were experts in fields where she lacked knowledge. A writer herself, with a degree in English Studies, she was happy to admit that many of her employees knew a lot more about Communications than she did.

When people worked overtime, Lucy made sure they were rewarded. There were always muffins, coffee, and other snacks available in the office. When people worked late, Lucy made sure to stay with them, and then ordered meals for everyone.

She also offered incentives for employees who were top performers. Lucy made sure everyone got a chance to speak at meetings, and that everyone's input was taken seriously. If someone made negative remarks about what was said in a meeting, she quickly stepped in and asked the employees to respect each other's input. This was awkward at first, but people soon learned to respect how Lucy operated.

Employees and clients both enjoyed working with Lucy, and her company grew steadily, although not as fast as Jane's agency at first. Lucy also managed to attract talent from other companies, including her direct competitor, Jane's company.

Higher EQ Equals Higher Job Satisfaction

According to the study done by Tagoe and Quarshie in 2016 among nurses in Accra, Ghana, higher emotional intelligence can be connected to greater job satisfaction.

The study included 83 female and 37 male registered nurses from three public hospitals in Accra. The Schutte Self-Report Emotional Intelligence Inventory and the Job Satisfaction Survey were used to assess job satisfaction and emotional intelligence.

The findings showed a correlation between emotional intelligence and job satisfaction among nurses of both genders. As discussed previously, emotional intelligence is the ability to identify emotions, and understand and manage them in order to advance personal growth.

Since nurses play a vital role in delivering quality healthcare to patients, their job satisfaction is important. Since they are exposed to many stressful situations, it's also essential that they have psychological qualities such as emotional intelligence. If nurses become demotivated, it can lead to unfortunate consequences, such as the death of patients.

Job satisfaction is ultimately connected to lower staff turnover and employees who are also more engaged at work.

According to the meta-analysis that was done by Miao, Humphrey, and Qian in 2017, emotional intelligence helps employees improve their job satisfaction, as it increases their positive feelings and helps them improve their job performance. Organizations should incorporate emotional intelligence in their recruitment, as well as their training and development programs in order to produce productive and satisfied employees.

Key Takeaways

- Emotional intelligence has become a strong predictor of success in organizations.
- The research of psychologist Daniel Goleman and others has shown that emotional intelligence is an essential requirement for good leaders.
- If your company is aiming for long-term success, it will need to make an effort to make its employees feel psychologically safe. Your employees should be able to share input and their opinions without the fear of being put down in front of others.
- Higher emotional intelligence can also be connected to higher job satisfaction.
- Staff turnover will be lower if employees are satisfied with their jobs and they will also be more engaged at work.

Chapter 3:

Emotionally Intelligent Leadership

Emotional intelligence in a company needs to be well-established in the leadership team before it can influence the company culture. This is essential, as employees often mirror the behavior of management.

The Importance of Emotionally Intelligent Leadership

The business world has been through much uncertainty since the beginning of the COVID-19 pandemic in early 2020, which has been accompanied by repeated outbreaks. Geopolitical tension and its economic consequences have also impacted companies and their employees.

During this time, emotionally intelligent leadership has become increasingly important. This involves how leaders will understand and manage their own emotions, as well as those of others.

In an effort to improve the culture of emotional intelligence in their respective workplaces, leaders will have to improve their own emotional intelligence first.

Focus on Your Habits: How Emotionally Intelligent Leaders Operate

To become an emotionally intelligent leader, you will have to first learn to recognize your own thoughts and manage them. You need to change your behavior to focus on the most important activities that will benefit your company.

If you want to be an emotionally intelligent leader, you will have to be conscious of how your emotional state influences your team's decision-making and performance. You also need to be able to inspire confidence in your team and energize them.

Emotionally intelligent leaders use their emotions to achieve the outcomes they want to achieve. An emotionally intelligent leader should have enough self-awareness and should understand what self-regulation strategies help them manage their own emotions best. Understanding your emotions can help you solve problems, and will also boost your productivity. You are able to steer your thinking based on your feelings in order to make sure you perform optimally in a specific task.

For example, you might be feeling down, but you need to be able to perform and think creatively in a meeting, or workshop. You have certain strategies that you use to make sure you are more positive, and your energy levels increase so that you can perform at an optimal creative level.

As an emotionally intelligent leader, you have to understand that empathy toward others is cognitive, you have to understand what others are going through, and you have to be able to feel what they're feeling. If you ask your employees how they are feeling, they will need to trust you enough to understand that you really want to know what they are experiencing, and that you want to support them.

If you suspect that one of your employees is going through something, but they indicate that they are doing fine when you ask them about it, you will have to probe a bit more. You need to be sensitive to the emotions of the group of people you manage, and demonstrate genuine care for the people who report to you. The best leaders always pay attention to the human side of the business.

An emotionally intelligent leader will be aware of both what is said by their staff members, and also of what is not being said. If you become skilled at understanding what others are experiencing, you'll be able to pick up changes in facial expressions, as well as voice and body language. You will be able to form a clear picture of what's happening with a group of people, by "reading between the lines." You won't jump to conclusions, but instead you will investigate to understand underlying motivations.

Emotionally intelligent leaders understand how they influence the culture of their teams, and will be able to maintain a positive climate. If you are this type of leader, you will be able to encourage positive emotions in your team, which is important for good performance, conflict resolution, decision making, and good dynamics within the group.

By ensuring positive emotions in their team or department, emotionally intelligent leaders also promote a climate of psychological safety which encourages employees to be themselves at the office, as they trust their teammates and feel connected to them.

A leader with high EI also understands how complicated emotions can be, why people respond in certain ways, as well as what causes certain types of emotions.

You will have to be aware of the importance of emotional intelligence in your own leadership, and you will be open to developing your EI skills. It's vital that you challenge yourself to develop your perspective and learn more emotional intelligence skills, even if it means you must face discomfort.

Developing EI is a process, and it can be difficult because we see our actions according to what our intentions are. However, we also see other people's actions according to the effect they have on us.

Case Study: Emotionally Intelligent Leadership

Adam has noticed that the behavior of Brandon, his star web developer, has changed over recent weeks. It's not that noticeable at first, but Brandon comes to the office with dark circles under his eyes, and he has stopped shaving. He also becomes quiet at meetings until he entirely stops giving input. Brandon becomes increasingly quiet and stops joking around with his colleagues as he used to do.

As a new manager, Adam is not sure how to approach the situation and decides to leave it for the moment. Brandon's work is still of high quality, but Adam becomes increasingly worried when he sees him eating takeout lunches at his desk, and hardly getting up during the day. Brandon only used to eat healthy lunches that his wife used to pack for him. Adam also notices that he is gaining a lot of weight around his middle.

Adam approaches Brandon in the kitchen while he is making coffee and starts chatting with him in a casual way. He asks Brandon how he is doing, but Brandon only answers in monosyllables, telling him that he is doing fine. Adam doesn't push the issue then, since Brandon is also a few years older than him, and he doesn't want to appear disrespectful.

However, he becomes increasingly worried when Brandon also gets involved in a confrontation with another staff member. Adam's boss, Louise, finally calls him to her office to complain about the deteriorating quality of Brandon's work. One of the company's biggest clients is threatening to take its work elsewhere after one of Brandon's projects failed.

After discussing the issue with Louise—who is firm, but understanding—Adam invites Brandon for coffee and a private discussion. He starts off by slowly prodding Brandon about his situation. Brandon is reluctant to say anything and becomes increasingly irritated. Adam puts more pressure on him. He wants to get to the root of the problem before Brandon really gets angry and walks out. He used to be close to Brandon when they were students before their ways parted, and they went their different ways for some years before they ended up working together again. He knows a little bit about Brandon's private life, and knows he married Sue, a girl who studied with them. Adam decides to change his tactics, and asks Brandon about Sue and his home life.

Brandon frowns and there are tears in his eyes. It turns out Sue had left him some months before, taking along their little daughter Alison. The situation had gone from bad to worse, and now she was insisting on a divorce.

After commiserating with him, Adam suggests to Brandon that he should take a leave of absence to sort out his home life. He also gives him the name of a psychologist that he himself had used in the past.

Brandon thanks Adam for his support and tells him that he will let him know if he needs support in the future.

Key Takeaways

- The business world has been through much uncertainty since the beginning of the COVID pandemic in early 2020. Emotionally intelligent leadership has become increasingly important during this time.

- In an effort to improve the culture of emotional intelligence in their workplaces, leaders will have to improve their own emotional intelligence first, as their employees will emulate their behavior.

- If you want to be an emotionally intelligent leader, you will have to be conscious of how your emotional state influences your team's decision-making and performance.

Improving Your Emotional Intelligence as a Leader

The reality is that you will have to consider your own level of emotional intelligence before you can make it an integral part of your organization. You need to be able to recognize what is responsible for your feelings, thoughts and behavior, and how you can adapt to focus on the most important activities.

Emotional Foundation

Our emotional foundation for the rest of our lives is already created in childhood. Unfortunately, we may have baggage from childhood, especially if we were abused or neglected as children. We could have learned to repress our feelings in childhood, especially if our parents weren't sympathetic toward our negative feelings, or we may even have been punished for displaying certain emotions such as anger.

When we are adults, we may experience negative feelings that are based on our childhood experiences. However, even if it's unconsciously, we may still be scared that we will be punished for expressing our feelings, like when we were children.

Especially if you are in a management position, it's important that you realize you may be transferring negative feelings you have for your childhood caretakers onto other people. This may cause relationship problems at work, for example with your employees, or your manager. You need to deal with the phenomenon of transference, by analyzing it as a consequence of what you experienced during your childhood.

In an effort to improve your emotional intelligence and manage your emotions, you need to confront the fear you have of your childhood caregivers. You need to realize what happened, and why it is causing you to act in a certain way now. Then you need to resolve to change your actions and behavior.

The renowned psychotherapist, Alice Miller, maintains that one of the main reasons for the violence we experience in the world today is because children have to suppress their rage during childhood when they might receive corporal punishment or abuse at the hands of their parents (Miller, 2015). When we are angry or sad as children, we often receive the message that this emotion shouldn't be displayed, and that we should 'grow up' and move on.

As a result of how you were treated during childhood, you may have formed negative beliefs about yourself. You may think there is something wrong with you or that you are unlovable. You could also see yourself as someone who is over-sensitive.

Some adults even become stuck in their psychological development and will keep acting in unsuitable ways, until they are able to get in touch with their childhood emotions.

Emotional Recognition and Management

If you understand your emotional history since childhood, it will help you understand yourself better as an adult. You will be able to recognize your emotions and act according to your needs. You will also be able to build better relationships at work and in your private life, as well as set strong boundaries so as not to be abused by other people.

You may also have never learned in childhood how to recognize, name, and manage your emotions. Many parents are unintentionally emotionally neglectful, as they never learned these skills themselves as children.

For example, let's look at Ben's situation. His parents never tried to help him identify what he was feeling or paid much attention to his emotions. When he cried because he got hurt, or someone mistreated him at school, he was often told to stop crying, as boys aren't supposed to cry.

Ben spent most of the week at school and also engaged in various after-school activities. His parents usually worked late, and the family had many commitments over the weekends. Ben was often left with a babysitter when he was a young child. His parents mostly treated him in a friendly, but superficial manner. He usually got everything he asked for from them.

Ben's parents never tried to form deeper relationships with him by talking about his feelings. He never learned the skills that would help him become emotionally aware as an adult. Ben learned to ignore his emotions and even became ashamed of them. He struggled to form relationships with other people, and his staff members regarded him as a cold and unfeeling boss. Ben was perfectionistic and placed impossible demands on his staff. He only realized he needed help after his wife left him, and he decided he needed to change if he still wanted to be part of his children's lives.

Ben had his own defense mechanisms when it came to displaying emotions. This behavior also had a negative effect on his role as a manager.

He blamed and judged his staff when things went wrong at the office. He found it difficult to relax around people, and often changed the topics of conversations to what he wanted them to be. Like his parents, he also chose work over intimacy, and his wife and children saw very little of him. He never spent much time with them, as there were always more important things to attend to at the office.

If you've been emotionally neglected as a child, you may still suffer from the after-effects as an adult. You may feel emotionally numb, and perhaps different from other people in ways you don't understand.

Do you find it difficult to understand your feelings and how they work? As an adult, you can take ownership of your feelings and how they work. Your emotions carry important messages between your brain and body, such as that you need to avoid something (fear), and that an interaction with another person has made you upset (anger).

It's essential that you learn how to manage your emotions and deal with past issues, as your emotions can shape your life choices and overall wellness. Emotional intelligence can also influence how well you do in your career. If you feel there are issues you need to overcome before you can work on your emotional intelligence, you should consider doing some introspection about your childhood.

Childhood Introspection

You will need to look at your childhood in an honest way to be able to make changes to your current situation. This will help you identify if your needs for approval, affection, attention, and affirmation were met by your caregivers. Once you can identify which of your needs weren't satisfied, you can work toward satisfying them yourself as an adult.

Realizing that you think and behave in certain ways as a result of your past will also help you break cycles of negative self-talk and will prevent you from sabotaging yourself in different situations—for example, stressful situations at work. If you can accept the truth about your past and change your mindset, it will assist you in healing any childhood trauma you might still be going through as an adult.

Doing some soul-searching about your childhood can help you discover and accept your authentic self. You get to put aside the expectations and ambitions put onto you by society. Your values will change as you become more of your authentic self, and you start to look within to determine what is important to you.

You can also work toward overcoming self-loathing in the forms of low self-esteem and self-criticism, by looking back at your past and where these feelings originated. You will gain self-confidence when you consider that you are now an adult and you don't have to feel them any longer. It should be easier to decide what you want and need from life.

Introspection will not only help you see yourself in a different way, it will also help you change the way in which you treat yourself:

- By helping you become more conscious of your own needs and wants.
- By allowing you to like and love yourself.
- By helping you be kinder to yourself and treat yourself with compassion.

You will be able to improve your relationships with everyone in your life and set healthier boundaries in your relationships.

Key Takeaways

- Our emotional foundation for the rest of our lives is formed in childhood. We may carry emotional baggage from our childhood with us for the rest of our lives, especially if we were abused or neglected during childhood.

- If you understand your emotional history since childhood, it will help you understand yourself better as an adult, and you should be able to recognize your emotions and form better relationships.

- You need to learn to manage your emotions and deal with past issues, as your emotions can shape your life choices and overall wellness.

- Conducting some introspection into your childhood will help you break cycles of negative self-talk. You will learn more about why you behave in certain ways, which will prevent you from sabotaging yourself in different situations, for example, when you are at work.

- Your childhood introspection can assist you to overcome low self-esteem. It will help you gain self-confidence, and you will realize what you need and want from life.

Improving Emotional Intelligence in the Workplace

Every employee in the workplace should be aiming to improve their emotional intelligence.

If we experience too much stress in our daily lives, we will show a lack of emotional intelligence and empathy in our behavior. We need to rest, exercise, and practice self-care if we want to remain empathetic to those around us.

However, not all stress is negative. Stress has helped the human species survive, as one of its main functions is to make us aware of physical danger.

Stress is now grouped into two categories, namely eustress and distress.

Eustress and Distress

The term 'stress' has mainly negative connotations, but stress is actually just the body's response to changes that place demands on it.

The body can perceive a change or threat as a stressor. Stress was necessary in the Stone Age for the survival of humans, and the fight or flight response enabled our ancestors to fight or run away from danger.

During this stress response, your heartbeat speeds up, your blood pressure increases, and you breathe faster. Your blood sugar level is raised to send more energy to your muscles and to help your mind to focus. The stress we experience today is mostly not external, but from within ourselves. Modern stress is mostly caused by psychological tension; for example when you are facing job demands, or you have to write an exam.

Eustress

Eustress is a fairly new term and refers to the motivating and positive type of stress. Eustress motivates you to achieve your goals and to continue striving to improve your performance, even when you face challenges.

Both types of stress activate the fight or flight response. One of the main differences between the two types of stress is that energy is released in a more haphazard manner in the case of distress.

When do you experience eustress and distress? It depends a lot on how you see yourself, and the stressor. If you feel you can overcome the stressor, you are more likely to experience it as eustress or positive stress. This will help you channel your energy to work on a solution to the stressor. Just be aware that eustress can turn into distress if the situation becomes overwhelming, or other stressors are happening at the same time. If you experience this, you will need to learn stress management techniques.

Distress

Distress is the negative stress that makes you feel anxious and overwhelmed. You can experience a range of symptoms such as irritability, headaches, tension, or insomnia.

Chronic distress can lead to illness and the development of mental health disorders. It will also affect the quality of the work you do, and your ability to manage your normal day-to-day life.

You can experience distress when you feel the stress in your life is not under your control, and you are not able to do anything to improve the situation.

Sources of distress could include a lack of money, being a victim of violent crime or living in a war zone, dissatisfaction with your job, illness, sleeping problems, and relationship problems, to name a few.

If you're exposed to distress for an extended period of time, you may struggle to function normally at home, and at work. There is a risk that you can develop anxiety and depression, or become addicted to substances.

Ways You Can Prevent Distress and Promote Eustress

It's possible to protect yourself against many of the negative effects of distress while using strategies to turn some of your stress into eustress.

These strategies will protect you against some of the worst effects of distress:

- Focus on parts of the situation that you can control. You would normally experience distress when you feel you are unable to cope with something. There is no point in feeling distressed about things you can't control. The only thing you are able to control is how you react to a situation. Consider if there are steps you can take to reduce your stress or that might even solve the problem.
- You should try to find meaning in stressful situations. It may be very hard to find anything positive in difficult situations, but people who do so are more likely to experience their stressor as eustress.
- Finding meaning in pain indicates that a person is resilient and resourceful. The situation could have given you new insights about yourself and your general situation in life, make it clearer

to you what matters most, or help you feel confident that you are able to overcome adversity. You can possibly even gain new opportunities from the situation if you look at it in a positive way.

- Identify steps you can take to improve the situation or prevent the outcome from being bad. Try to determine if there is anything you can do to improve the situation. Even if the outcome is not what you desired, you will feel better because you made an effort to change the outcome.

- Be kind to yourself. While you are experiencing distress, you may be inclined to blame yourself for things you didn't do, or set unrealistic expectations for yourself. Self-compassion is more motivational than self-criticism. People who are kind to themselves are less likely to fail, and they tend to keep on trying when they fail, instead of giving up.

- You need to address the root cause of distress in your life. This could be a relationship in your life, your job, or even bad habits that you have developed, such as drinking too much every night. If the root cause of stress is in your life, you need to work on this issue to make positive changes, or if this is impossible, you need to distance yourself from it.

- Use mindfulness to be present in your life. Many people spend a lot of time either worrying about the past or the future. These efforts are unproductive, as you can't predict the future, and you also can't change the past. You can free yourself from this by focusing your attention on the present. Make an effort to bring your attention back to the present when you find your mind wandering to unhelpful and negative thoughts.

- Increase your physical exercise so that you have an outlet for stress. Moving your body is a great way to relieve stress, and helps you rebalance your hormones and the chemicals in your body. You should make exercise a priority during times when you experience high stress. Exercise will sharpen your mind and help you calm down. This will also improve your performance. You may need professional help if you experience intense, ongoing stress as this can have serious health consequences in the long-term.

- Reach out to friends and family you can trust during times you experience high distress. Ask for the help and support you need.

- You can try relaxation techniques like yoga, deep breathing, and muscle relaxation. The Emotional Freedom Technique (EFT) tapping is also a good way to reduce your stress levels. Tap your fingers on different energy points in your body, while saying positive affirmations aloud. This technique can be done in 10 to 15 minutes daily and is highly effective.

Key Takeaways

- The term 'stress' has negative connotations, but stress is actually just the body's response to changes that create demands on it.

- Eustress refers to the positive type of stress. Eustress motivates you to achieve your goals and to continue striving to improve your performance, even when you face challenges.

- Distress is the negative stress that makes you feel anxious and overwhelmed.

How Managers Can Prevent

Burnout

The problem of burnout is becoming increasingly prevalent in businesses around the globe. Managers could easily become victims of burnout if they don't put their mental health first.

A management skill you need to have is the ability to delegate successfully. This will reduce your stress levels, and hopefully save you from burnout.

How to Delegate and Reduce Your Stress Levels

If you want to accomplish your goals as a manager, you will have to learn to delegate successfully. This means that you will have to stop doing some of the more technical work you were doing previously, in order to pay more attention to performance managing your staff.

When it comes to delegation, you assign the responsibilities of a task to a staff member, but you are still the one who will be held accountable for the task. You will need to decide how much autonomy you will give the staff member to work on the task, and how much control you will take over the process. This could also depend on the available time, and how much experience the staff member has.

When you are already overwhelmed and stressed, you may experience the following challenges when you want to delegate to staff:

- You don't trust someone else to do the task, and you think you don't have time to train them to do it properly.
- You think it's faster just to do most things yourself.

- You are worried your team doesn't have the right skills to do the task, and you may have to re-do it anyway.

The reality is that you will have to change your mindset about delegating. You will have to give people a chance to learn, otherwise, nothing will change and you will continue being overwhelmed.

You will have to invest time to mentor and train your staff so that they are prepared when you delegate to them. You need to have a long-term view of delegation.

Don't dump mundane tasks on people, rather, try to give them a full project that they can see through from beginning to end, as they will find this more satisfying. It is also a much better learning process when it comes to understanding all the processes in a certain department.

The Benefits of Delegating

Delegating can be beneficial for both you and your staff, in the following ways:

- Staff members can learn more skills, which will help them feel more engaged with their work, and they will be less likely to leave your company.
- It can help your employees become more self-sufficient over time, which means you will spend less time providing them with support.
- It can improve the trust between you and your staff.
- You will be less overworked if you surround yourself with capable people who are able to handle the tasks you delegate to them.
- Your company's service to your clients should also improve if you have more qualified employees available to deliver the service.

How to Delegate Effectively

Follow these steps to make sure you delegate effectively:

- Analyze your time and consider what tasks you can delegate to your staff members. Break your tasks down, and delegate some of them. Try to expose your staff to meaningful tasks and processes.
- Make sure that you develop your staff members, so that they can step into your shoes when needed. You should take certain things into account such as the current skill levels of staff, their current workload and the skills they want to develop, as well as how tasks are currently distributed among them. Consider the big picture before you start delegating work. Avoid choosing the high performers every time you delegate, as they will eventually suffer from burnout, and other staff members won't get the opportunity to develop. This could cause staff members who are never selected for tasks to become disengaged with their work, and they might end up eventually leaving the company.
- Make sure you brief the staff member properly when you delegate to them. Give them the details and tell them why the task is being delegated to them. Create a checklist for them with clear objectives that have to be met. Inform them about what resources are available to them, such as equipment and human resources. Also provide them with milestones and points at which they should check in with you. Describe to them how they should do the tasks; this is less important if they are more experienced.
- To make sure they understand the tasks, ask them to summarize what they must do in their own words. Offer them support if and when they need it, and get a commitment from them.

- Monitor and encourage staff while they are busy with the task. Don't be overbearing, but also be available if people need advice.
- Finally, give the staff member some feedback after the task has been completed. This will help them grow and learn.

Other Habits That Can Help You Relieve Your Stress

As a manager, you will usually experience even more stress than the other employees. Managers need to be able to focus, adapt, and also be accountable. Your higher stress levels could also put you at risk of mental health conditions such as anxiety and depression, as well as chronic conditions such as high blood pressure.

You won't be able to get rid of stress entirely, but you can manage it, and prevent negative emotions and ill health from dominating your life.

- Identify your triggers. What do you stress about? Consider how your stress levels change throughout the day. Do you at times feel more anxious and irritable, or less patient and even tenser?
- Determine the main cause of your feelings. If you find that certain situations or people place stress on you, you will have to find new ways of dealing with them.
- Use activities such as mindfulness meditation to relieve your stress. Exercise, deep breathing, and music could also help you out.
- You need to realize that aiming for perfection is not doing anyone any favors. As a manager, you are responsible for making sure everything goes well, but being a perfectionist has all kinds of negative connotations. It could cause procrastination among your staff members, as they will be scared to do things wrong, and it could also lead to friction between management and staff. You need to come up with more reasonable priorities for yourself and your team.

- Don't ignore your problems. Instead, talk to people who are part of your support network. It's a bad idea to ignore your stress, as it will just become worse. Reach out to people you can talk to, whether they are family, friends, or coworkers. Talk about your stress levels and what causes most of your stress. Even just talking about it may make you feel better, and help you to manage your stress. Your loved ones could make recommendations on how you can deal with your stress in healthy ways. This is better than suppressing your stress.

- Try to lead a healthier lifestyle, whether you are a manager or just an ordinary staff member. This involves getting enough sleep, eating healthy meals, drinking enough water, as well as getting exercise. A healthy lifestyle will also improve your mood, and you will be able to resist stress better.

- Managerial responsibilities can, in many circumstances, be unnecessary. You may think of it as your job to make sure the work is done in what you think is the best possible way. However, the best manager is often not the one who is actively managing people and tasks. They are often the person who is adaptable and can work well with their colleagues. If you think more of yourself as a collaborator, you will also find that you tend to stress less.

- Don't take on too much work, and acknowledge when you need help. You shouldn't be doing everything by yourself, and it's essential that you delegate to your team members.

First-Time Managers

As a first-time manager, you are especially susceptible to burnout, as you are also on a steep learning curve. Being promoted to management is a significant career change and you will experience all kinds of changing dynamics at work. If you don't look after your mental health, you could develop burnout, which could also rub off on your team.

There are several ways in which new managers can manage burnout.

As a new manager, you may feel that you are under pressure to get things right and prove yourself to everyone around you. However, you have to realize that if you are a perfectionist, it can lead to negative behavior like micromanagement and hovering. Perfectionist tendencies can make it difficult for you and your team to achieve your goals.

Expecting everyone on your team to adhere to an unrealistic standard of excellence can actually demotivate them, rather than push them to do better. Instead, refocus your priorities. Be clear about the quality of work you expect. Then ask people what they need from you, in order for them to do that work on their own. Establishing reasonable goals will help your team become more autonomous and feel accountable for their tasks.

You will need to ask people what they will need from you to do the work on their own as well as they possibly can. Set reasonable goals and help people become accountable for your work.

While it may seem essential to speak to your team regularly, one of the ways to reduce micromanagement is to reduce how often you meet with your team. Employees tend to feel less like they are being micromanaged if they have to meet with their supervisors less. Meetings also keep employees away from completing their tasks, and can lead to more stress. If you have to meet with your staff members, only do it when it's absolutely necessary. For example, arrange a meeting with them when you need to review work that has been completed. You can use tools like Slack or Monday.com to update or organize work.

It might be difficult to ask for help, but as a first-time manager, you might sometimes find that you are in over your head. You are still trying to find your feet and earn the respect of your team. If you get too anxious and stressed, you could be on the road to burnout. This is also unfair to your team, and might have a negative effect on productivity.

When people in management positions speak about struggles and problems they experience at work, such as becoming overwhelmed, it creates a safe space for other staff members to do the same, and this will contribute to creating a psychologically safe workspace for everyone. Employees need a safe space where they can speak about their daily challenges, without feeling shame or guilt.

Employees are usually also more willing to go above and beyond for managers who are open and show vulnerability—so be honest with your teammates, and share with your staff how you feel. For example, let them know if you are excited or apprehensive about the day.

If things go wrong, have an honest discussion with your team members. Discuss what you learned from the situation, and what you are going to do to avoid such issues in the future.

Key Takeaways

- Managers could become victims of burnout if they don't prioritize their mental health.

- Delegating successfully can reduce your stress levels, saving you from burnout.

- You will have to train and prepare your staff for when you delegate to them.

- Staff members will learn new skills and become more self-sufficient when you delegate to them.

- First-time managers are also susceptible to burnout, as they face a steep learning curve.

Practice Mindfulness

When you are a manager working with people, you need to be able to manage your emotions. Mindfulness can help you detach yourself from your thoughts and feelings. As a leader, this is an essential skill that you have to master.

What Is Mindfulness in the Workplace?

Mindfulness is about being focused and present in the moment. You are not distracted by what work you still need to complete later today, or what happened at the meeting last week. Being mindful allows you to fully concentrate on the task you are busy with. This is a useful and essential skill, as we have to deal with such a magnitude of information every day.

Benefits of Mindfulness in the Workplace

It's good to be aware of the benefits of mindfulness in the workplace, especially if you have to convince other staff members or managers of the benefits.

The benefits of mindfulness in the workplace can be described as follows:

- Mindfulness can help build resilience among staff, and meditation can also help lessen the effects of stress and anxiety. It can also improve the ability to be productive under stress.
- It has been shown that mindfulness can also increase emotional intelligence. It can also help us regulate our emotions and improve our levels of patience. It's easier to cope when things don't go well if you have an inner reserve of calm. You will also

be more equipped to deal with workplace disagreements, and you will be less inclined to react in an emotional way.

- Mindfulness can also help staff to be more creative. If we are more relaxed as a result of being mindful, we give ourselves the opportunity to be more creative. Mindfulness also helps with out-of-the-box innovative thinking.

- It can also improve personal relationships in the workplace. Interpersonal relationships can become strained in the workplace as a result of stress, anger, and anxiety. Mindfulness techniques that include meditation can make us more tolerant of each other and help us forge positive personal connections with our colleagues.

- Mindfulness can also help you focus better. It's natural for your mind to wander, and there are also many distractions on a daily basis, such as phone calls, constant email notifications, or colleagues coming to your office to talk about a query. For this reason, it can be difficult to remain focused on a task. Mindfulness can help you improve your ability to concentrate.

You should note that mindfulness should be voluntary, and employees shouldn't feel that they're being pressured to take part in it. Employees should be able to opt- out if they want to. It's just one of the tools to promote employee wellness.

Mindfulness is also not aimed at increasing productivity in the office. The idea is to promote different ways of thinking, and as a by-product. productivity may improve.

Being a Mindful Manager

Creating a mindful office environment can also boost employee productivity. It can take time to integrate mindfulness into your daily routine, and one of the first things you need to practice as a mindful manager is allowing yourself to go about your day free from judgment.

Being a mindful manager involves reacting objectively to situations and becoming aware of your positive and negative judgments. This will allow you to evaluate situations, as they really are more effective.

If you look objectively at problems employees are raising, you can reframe challenges into opportunities. Another mindful way of managing is to look at a project in its individual steps instead of only the end goal, as it then becomes a daunting task.

In the process of being mindful, being patient with yourself and others is of the utmost importance. It's also important to view the present as it is, without being judgmental. You also need to be able to accept realistic timelines, which will relieve employees' anxieties of being expected to deliver beyond what they are capable of delivering.

A patient manager who deals well with employee frustrations and other workplace problems can bring a calm and focused mindset to their team.

Remember that you don't have to know everything, or have all the answers. It's an important attribute of a good manager to be able to recognize great ideas from your employees, even the new ones.

The core idea behind being a mindful manager is that you must be able to let go. You need to step away from the idea that things only need to be done in a certain way. There will be issues, but if you can let go of the idea that you have to be in control of everything, it will relieve your stress, and that of your employees. It will also foster a culture of understanding and boost productivity.

Practical Ways of Introducing Mindfulness

Before you introduce mindfulness, you need to be aware that some employees are going to be against the idea from the start. However, once they have had a chance to experience some of the techniques—such as meditation—themselves, they may start to feel differently about the project.

Quiet Spaces

Employees need quiet spaces to meditate if they feel like doing so. Not everyone will want to meditate, but other staff members can use the quiet spaces to refocus their thoughts without the distraction of phones, emails, and office chatter. The company could also consider playing relaxing or classical music in these spaces.

Mandatory Breaks

Make sure staff take mandatory regular breaks, including a lunch break. Under pressure, some people will keep going without eating lunch or drinking coffee, but this pace can't be sustained for a long time, and it's detrimental to physical and mental health. A mindfulness program needs to make staff aware of how important it is to take short breaks, as well as their lunch break. You will be able to concentrate better on your work, even if you only manage to take a 20-minute break.

If you switch off your phone and walk around the block, you have already had a refreshing break. Taking time away from your desk to eat, rather than gobbling down a sandwich at your desk, is a good way to enhance mindfulness, as well as your overall well-being. Another idea is to schedule five-minute breaks after meetings to help staff refocus themselves for the next task.

Gratitude

We have a tendency to focus on things that go wrong in the workplace, rather than things that have gone well. As part of mindfulness, it's an excellent idea to actively practice gratitude. Encourage staff members to write down what they are grateful for at the end of every day. You can gradually train your brain to be more positive, and an optimistic outlook will have a positive effect on work.

Mindfulness Exercises

You can begin by encouraging employees to do short mindful exercises. This will enable them to start the day with the right attitude. If they had a long commute or spent a sleepless night with sick children, they may need to be reenergized before they can focus on work and the challenges that may be ahead for the day.

Mindfulness exercises will help them clear their minds and refocus their energy to help them do their best at work.

Start with a ten-minute exercise where you need to sit upright, close your eyes, and relax. Focus on your breathing, including every breath that comes in and goes out. If other thoughts keep creeping in, count to three every time you exhale. Enjoy the calmness of this time. This exercise will help staff focus better and start their day with the right mindset.

You can also do the following mindfulness exercises:

- Encourage people to actively listen to each other, and give each other their undivided attention. Don't check your emails, or your phone messages while you are talking to each other. You should make eye contact when you are speaking to each other. Don't assume that you know what another person is going to say, and also don't think of a reply while they are still speaking to you. Try to process what someone is trying to tell you, in a non-judgemental way.
- You can also practice mindfulness at work, by being grateful for things that you usually take for granted. Try to think of five things every time you do this exercise. It can be simple things, such as the coffee shop near your office that sells affordable cappuccinos.
- Practice mindful breathing at your desk, by standing up or sitting down for one minute. Just focus on your breathing during this time. Inhale air slowly through your nose, and

exhale slowly out your mouth. Focus on the different sensations in your body while you do so. Put your hands on your belly and chest to feel your breathing. Feel your body taking in positive energy as you exhale.

- Try mindful eating while you are at work. Eat slowly; taste and enjoy your food. We are often in a hurry, and we eat too fast if we eat while we are sitting at our desks.

- Try mindful eating away from your desk, as it can improve your digestion, and it will also prevent you from overeating.

- Your aim should be to focus mindfully on your work. Forget about multitasking, as this is stressful and just leads to errors. In the long run, multitasking actually leads to getting less done. Just concentrate on what you are doing at the moment, and forget about other distractions.

- Immerse yourself mindfully in your projects to really experience what you are doing at the moment. Instead of rushing to get your work done, you should concentrate while you are working, and enjoy what you are doing. For example, you can practice this even while doing a routine job such as washing dishes at home. Focus on how the water feels on your hands, how the soap smells, and the noise made by the running water.

- The idea is to be happy and satisfied in the moment, no matter what you are doing. You can even discover ways to immerse yourself creatively in a routine task.

- Another interesting exercise is mindful listening. The aim of this is to listen to sounds without being judgmental. Find music that you have never listened to before, and listen to it through headphones with closed eyes. Listen to every sound while isolating the different instruments. Try to also isolate the vocals. Listen to the sounds objectively and try to remain neutral. Just hear the sounds without thinking about everything you are hearing.

- Try to get some form of exercise during your breaks at work, such as walking or running. Concentrate on how it feels when your body moves. Enjoy the feeling of the air on your skin, and become aware of the smells and sounds around you.

- Look at a natural object as if it's the first time you are seeing it. It could be a flower, insect, stone, or any type of natural object. Appreciate the place it has in the natural order of things. Make sure you explore every aspect of it. This exercise can also help you connect with nature.

- Do some stretches when you get a chance, and notice how your body feels. You could even do this while waiting in line somewhere.

- Do this exercise if you feel you are getting caught up in your thoughts. Take five deep, slow breaths, and notice how the air moves through your body. Look around you and notice five things you can see. Also, pay attention to five things you can hear, and then five things you can feel in contact with your body. This could be the feeling of clothes against your skin or your feet on the ground. Finish this exercise by taking five more slow breaths.

You can use apps such as Calm (https://www.calm.com/) and HeadSpace (https://www.headspace.com/) to help you with your meditation exercises.

Key Takeaways

- Mindfulness can help you learn how to manage your emotions, which is an essential skill you need to have as a leader.

- Mindfulness is about being focused and present in the moment.

- The core idea behind being a mindful manager is that you must be able to let go. There is more than one acceptable way of doing things.

- Doing mindfulness exercises can help you start your day with the right mindset.

Time to Reflect

As a business leader, you need to create time in your schedule for reflection every day. You need 20 to 30 minutes every day to think about what worked well and what didn't. What were your thoughts and emotions, and how did they affect your performance as a leader?

As a manager, your day might be full of solving crises and problems, replying to emails and attending meetings, and coaching staff members. The idea of setting time aside for thinking might sound somewhat impossible. However, if you can take some time to think, you can actually improve your team's productivity. Sometimes you need to take a step away, and remove yourself from what is directly in front of you. You need to be able to see who is doing well, and who might need help.

If you take a step back, you will also start to see trends, and you will be able to think more strategically.

Daily self-reflection will strengthen your awareness and will also enable you to make better choices. However, to learn and improve, you need to see things as they really are, and not only in a positive light, like social media posts. You will only really be able to learn and grow when you can acknowledge your mistakes to yourself and your team members.

If you can be honest with yourself when you reflect, it will help you with making decisions, as well as learning and communicating more effectively. The more you practice, the more you will make progress.

Practicalities of Your Self-Reflection

You need to decide what time of the day will be the best for your self-reflection. First thing in the morning, when your mind is still clear, could be a good option. This will also help you prioritize what is important for the day before your phone starts to ring and you receive lots of emails. You could also reflect on your day in the evening before you go to bed. The idea is to make time when you can be honest with yourself.

Good ways to do self-reflection can be to do it while walking, writing in a journal, or simply sitting with your eyes closed.

You also need to consider how you can use your time effectively while reflecting. If you're left-brained, you will tend to be more methodical, while right-brained creatives might prefer to write down their thoughts as they come to them in a journal.

Reflection Activity

The following activities will hopefully make your reflection time a bit easier and more productive.

- Take five minutes to write down the positive and negative emotions you felt throughout the day. You should reflect on this list at the end of the week.
- Consider how you managed your behavior during the times you experience this behavior.
- Did your emotions reflect your decision-making or your relationships at work? Did you do anything against your personal values when faced with these emotions?

- You can analyze your feelings and behavior by using columns. In one column, write about the event that took place. Supply some details about the event (what happened, and where were you? Who was involved?).

- In the next column, write about your emotions (which emotions did you experience? How intense were the emotions you experienced, on a scale from 0 to 10?).

- In the last column, write your negative thoughts (what were you thinking, and what could be the reason that you thought in this way?).

Key Takeaways

- You need to reflect on your day for 20 to 30 minutes at the end of each evening.

- You need to take a step back to think about what is working and what is not.

- Daily self-reflection will strengthen your awareness and help you make better decisions.

Show an Interest in Your Employees

As part of creating a psychologically safe work environment, you need to make an effort to really get to know your employees, and also to some extent what they are like in their personal lives. It will be valuable to find out how they like to spend their spare time and what their values are. If you show an interest in your staff members, it can build trust between you, as well as a good working relationship.

The trick is to show your employees you value them more than simply as workers who can be replaced. Try to think of something you value about every employee. Show your employees that you care about their personal lives, and their partners, by inviting them to company events. You don't have to socialize with your employees, but they need to know you care about them as people.

You can also decide how you want employees to see you, and then act according to that. You may decide that you want to appear somewhat stoic and closed-off to maintain the respect of your staff, but you will regret it if you are avoiding making any personal connection with them.

If you don't connect with your employees at all, you are not going to have a dedicated team for the long-term. Employees who feel valued and appreciated are more likely to go the extra mile for their employer.

Even if you don't want to be too closely connected with your employees, it's essential to show them you care. Help your employees where you can, not only with work issues, but even personal ones, if needed. For example, if you know an employee is looking for a place to rent closer to work, see if there is any way that you can help them find one. If you help someone in a difficult situation, you will be repaid with their loyalty.

Do your best to relate to your employees, and don't act like you are more important than they are. Showing your vulnerability and imperfections to your employees can also strengthen your connection with them.

Support your employees and back them up with difficult clients. In the long run, your most talented employees will be worth more to you than a well-paying, but rude client.

Also, be honest and transparent when you give feedback to your employees. Don't be unkind to people, but also be sure not to shield them from the truth. Transparent feedback will get better results in the long-term.

Make time to speak to your employees regularly. They won't feel appreciated if you're always too busy to talk to them. Hold yourself accountable to have one-on-one sessions with your team members.

Send your team thank you notes or emails to show your appreciation. Also, encourage them when you're working on big projects. Tell them in a few sentences why you value them.

Pay attention to what your employees enjoy doing and where their interests lie. If they show an interest in other aspects of the business besides their job, create opportunities for them where they can get different experiences or job shadowing opportunities.

Your employees will only care about your company's long-term vision if they feel you see each of them as a valuable person. They need to feel that their manager and company are invested in them.

Other Ways You Can Show Your Employees You Care

There are other small ways that you can show your employees you appreciate them:

- Give them some time off or let them leave early. Tell them that you appreciate them for the hard work they have been doing, and you want them to have some time for themselves.
- You can give them gifts or bonuses to show them you appreciate their contribution to the company.
- Give compliments to specific people when they have done something well.
- Collaborate with your team members and don't micromanage them. Micromanaging just shows someone you don't trust them to do something right. Also, coach your employees, and don't boss them around.
- Trust your team members and they will trust you to do what is best for them.

Key Takeaways

- It's important that you make an effort to get to know your employees.

- If you show an interest in your staff members, it can build trust between you.

- Employees who feel valued and appreciated are more likely to go the extra mile for their employer.

- Show your employees in small ways that you appreciate them.

Building Trust

There are two types of trust that play an important role in the workplace.

Practical trust: Hard-working employees earn this trust by showing up every day on time and meeting all their deadlines. You will build up a reputation as being reliable and competent. If there is no trust, others may try to micromanage you, and productivity will suffer.

Emotional trust: You do more than is expected of you, and manage to create meaningful bonds with your team. You need to know how to network and build relationships.

It will take time to build trust with your team members, and you will have to work at this every day. You can build trust with your employees by doing what you say, and saying what you're going to do. Acknowledge when you are wrong, as it shows you are human, and this will help you gain trust. Also, admit when you don't have the answers.

When coworkers trust each other, it can make a big difference in the success of the workplace. As a manager, it's essential that you do your best to boost trust in your team.

If coworkers trust each other, they will feel confident and secure when they deal with each other. They will know who they can depend on and who is credible.

It's essential to build trust if you are going to be successful as a manager or employee. If you can build trust with someone, it means you make them comfortable relying on you, and they feel confident and motivated to work with you.

If coworkers trust each other, they are more motivated to work together on projects and enjoy doing so. A workplace with a lot of trust usually has a culture that has been developed through hard work and teamwork. A company will be more successful if there is trust in the workplace.

A Lack of Trust

A lack of trust can have a negative effect on the bottom line of the business. The retention of employees and achievement levels depend on building trust in teams. Employees won't stay in a work environment where they don't feel secure, and they also won't do their best for management they don't trust. The success of innovation and brainstorming also depend on coworkers trusting each other when it comes to presenting their ideas. Ideas that seem outrageous at first can often be the best, but people won't be confident to share them if there is no trust in the team.

You ultimately want to create a culture of productivity and trust in your business, as your bottom line is at stake.

Practical Ways in Which You Can Build Trust

If you want your team to feel comfortable about approaching you for help, and to appreciate your work, it is important that you build their trust.

One of the easiest ways to build trust is to do what you said you will and to follow through on your promises. If someone relies on you to finish a project, you will be breaking their trust by not completing what you are supposed to be doing. If you know you won't be able to do something because you don't have the skills, and you will run out of time, be honest with your teammates. Don't over-promise and then under-deliver.

Another way in which you can build trust with your team is to ensure you communicate effectively. If you send emails, make sure your email is friendly but professional. Be mindful of your tone, and make sure you don't send the wrong message. Listen actively when your coworkers communicate with you so that they know you are listening actively and that you value their words.

You can build trust with new employees by mentoring them. Show them around your office, and explain to them how your workplace functions. If your team becomes aware of your mentorship abilities, they may also become more confident in your work relationship.

Also, build trust by being honest at all times. This builds a culture of open communication.

It also builds trust if you show interest in your employees' personal lives. You may find that you work better together when you know at least something about your employees. You can also have welcome functions for new hires, and celebrate birthdays and other milestones at work.

Admit it if you have made a mistake, and how it influenced workplace operations. Admitting that you have done something wrong shows integrity, which will lead to trust.

It will also be easier to build trust if you are a more active part of the group. Do your best to interact with your coworkers during and after meetings. Offer to assist your coworkers if they are struggling with something.

Be patient while you build trust gradually. It can take a while to build trust within a group, so just continue being genuine and not too pushy.

It can build a great deal of trust if a manager admits they don't know something, and they have to rely on the expertise of coworkers.

You need to set the right expectations for staff. Set high expectations when it comes to the quality of work and client interactions. Hold your employees accountable. Be committed to your decisions, but also flexible in your approach. However, don't focus on strict rules that may seem important to you, but will break the trust with your employees. For example, you won't build trust when you scold employees for being a few minutes late, or for taking some time off when they need it.

It's a good idea to have team-building events from time to time, when possible. You don't have to do them face-to-face, as you can have virtual team exercises that could include some fun activities. You could give prizes to winners to encourage people to attend and have some friendly competition.

Ask for Feedback

Even if you feel your emotional intelligence is on a high level, it's a good idea to ask your employees for feedback. Different people will perceive you in different ways.

Do the following exercise, and ask your employees to rate your emotional intelligence abilities.

Choose five-ten employees who you trust, and who you know also trust you. Ask them to rate you anonymously on the following skills. The ratings should be from 0 (not at all) to 5 (completely).

- How good am I at active listening?
- Do I take the time to understand others?
- Have I invested in the personal and professional development of my employees?
- Do I act in a passionate and comparing way toward the people I lead?
- Do I take the time to get to know my employees and understand what they need?
- Am I skilled at persuading employees regarding ideas that I believe will help our business?

Ask employees to provide some explanation for their choices. This will give you an idea of what you need to improve.

Key Takeaways

- There are two types of trust that play an important role in the workplace; practical trust and emotional trust.

- Hard-working employees can earn practical trust by showing up every day on time and meeting all their deadlines. You will build a reputation as a competent and reliable employee.

- You do more than is expected and manage to create meaningful bonds with your team. This will lead to emotional trust.

- You can build trust through effective communication.

Should Employees Review Their Managers?

Asking your employees to review you is a good growth opportunity for you as a leader. Keep an open mind, and be willing to change if you realize this might be needed. Ask for anonymous feedback if you want their honest opinions. They might be scared to give feedback face-to-face, as they might be branded as trouble makers and have a bad attitude.

Employees need to feel their opinions matter, as they are much more likely to be engaged than if they feel they are just another number.

If you have an office discussion about the feedback you received, try not to come across as accusatory. Ask them specific questions; for instance, how they would feel if you change a certain tactic or sales process.

Criticism can be hard, but see it as an opportunity for you to grow and change.

Benefits of Asking for Feedback From Employees

You can find out what makes your employees happy at work, and what would be the ideal workplace for them. If you understand what they are looking for, you can take steps to create an environment that keeps them happy. It will also help keep your staff turnover low.

Getting feedback from employees ensures that your company has a culture of open communication, and it also gives you an idea of areas where you need to grow. Your employees can also give you a better idea of what you are doing right.

Practicing Empathy

Empathy can be defined as the ability to sense other people's emotions and be able to imagine what that person might be feeling or thinking.

Most of us will spend many hours at work during our lifetimes. Now imagine going to work every day in a hostile and unfriendly office. It would be extremely difficult to remain motivated and deliver your best work in an environment like this.

Empathy is one of the pillars on which a supportive office culture is built. Empathy can help you build rapport with your coworkers, management, and clients. It can also help you a great deal if you are working in a customer-centric business, to build a comfortable and authentic work environment.

We might not understand how to display empathy at work, but it's not that complicated. If you are the type of person who listens to your coworkers or clients when they come to you with a problem, and you are sensitive to their emotions, you are already an empathetic person.

Types of Empathy

Empathy is an integral part of emotional intelligence, as it helps you connect with your colleagues, loved ones, and friends. There are different ways to experience empathy.

Psychologists have defined three types of empathy: Cognitive, emotional and compassionate.

Cognitive Empathy

Cognitive empathy has to do with understanding what another person is thinking. Having cognitive empathy will help you when it comes to negotiations, understanding different viewpoints, and motivating other people. However, this type of empathy doesn't help you put yourself in someone else's shoes when it comes to sensing what they are feeling. You will be able to understand and comprehend what they feel, but it's not the same as feeling what they are experiencing.

For example, doctors and nurses are able to use cognitive empathy to understand what sick patients are experiencing. They can't afford to become emotionally involved.

Cognitive empathy is helpful in situations where you need to get into someone else's head to be able to interact in an understanding way with them. However, it may seem that, in order to truly understand another person's emotions, you need to be able to feel them yourself. People who only respond with cognitive empathy may seem too detached, or even cold.

Emotional Empathy

Emotional empathy involves physically feeling another person's emotions, almost as if that person's emotions are contagious. Someone who is an 'empath' is usually capable of taking on the emotional or mental state of another person.

Emotional empathy can be beneficial in close interpersonal relationships and careers like HR, marketing, and coaching. The negative side of emotional empathy is that it can overwhelm the person who is feeling the other person's emotions, and it can be inappropriate in certain circumstances.

Emotional empathy is usually a deep-seated, gut reaction that can be difficult to control. This is intimate and can help you form a strong bond with someone. However, if you struggle to manage your own distressing emotions, this can overwhelm you and lead to burnout. It can make even small interactions overwhelming.

Compassionate Empathy

Compassionate empathy is about understanding a person's situation, feeling with them, and also being moved to help them. This is the type of empathy we usually strive for.

Compassionate empathy takes the middle ground between cognitive empathy and emotional empathy. You can use your emotional intelligence to effectively respond to a situation with loving detachment. It's ideal, too, as you don't take on other people's burdens or feelings. You can even balance mindfulness with compassionate caring.

Social and Psychological Benefits of Empathy

If a person receives empathy, they will feel understood and less alone. Their anxiety will decrease, and they will be better able to find solutions to their problems.

The person who expresses empathy will feel useful and their self-confidence will increase. They will be able to express more authentic and intimate relationships with other people.

Understanding the negative emotions of other people can decrease the risk of negative behavior in the workplace. For example, if someone left a meeting, and you understand that this was a result of them being humiliated by someone else. You will then not see the person as unprofessional, and you'll be able to work with them again.

For example, if you understand feelings, you won't throw away items that belonged to your wife's late father, as you will understand they mean more to her, than just material items.

Can You Have Too Much or Too Little Empathy?

We learn empathy from our childhood caregivers. Adults need to respond to the child's needs consistently while setting limits, depending on the constraints of emotional and social life.

If the needs of other people aren't expressed well, or if no limits are put on what the child wants, they will find it difficult to put themselves into the place of other people.

As an adult, this person will struggle to understand and respond in an appropriate way to the needs of other people. This could cause conflicts in their professional and personal life, as well as problems in communicating with others.

The person who struggles to be empathetic will find themselves in a self-centered, objective and logical world, without access to the inner world of others, and won't experience intimacy as a result of this behavior. People who lack empathy often don't have access to their own feelings.

Some people are natural empaths and have no problem seeing things from the perspective of a colleague or friend. However, if empathy is at an extreme level, it could also be harmful.

If children are abused or suffer from attachment issues, they can find it difficult to deal with social and affective relationships. They spend a lot of time trying to be likable, as they lived with the fear of not being loved. Their main goal in life is then to understand the needs of their parents and to make them happy.

Children like this usually develop hypervigilance and are often anxious. They spend their childhood studying their parents' behavior in the hope of understanding them and finding ways to please them, in the hope that their parents will love them.

When these children become adults, they usually have high degrees of empathy, but also high levels of anxiety as they fear being abandoned, and they also usually develop low self-esteem.

Learning Empathy as an Adult

It's never too late to learn empathy to build better relationships with other people. You can follow these steps to develop your empathy:

- When you are talking to another person, look at their gestures, their posture and expressions, and the way they speak.
- Put your frame of reference and values aside when dealing with someone. Focus on the other person and their frame of reference.
- Try not to judge the feelings of others in a critical way. Don't question their feelings. Instead, see their feelings as authentic and valid.
- Pay attention to your own emotions, thoughts, and physical reactions.
- Try to think about what the other person is feeling and what you feel in response.

Therapy Can Help You Improve Your Empathy

In order to be empathetic to other people, you need to know your own emotions first. If you're empathetic, you're able to accept others with their differences. You want to know others and who they really are behind the facade they usually display to the world.

If you have never learned to identify and name your own emotions, it's going to be very difficult for you to recognize other people's emotions. Therapy can help you make progress in this regard. A psychotherapist can set up treatment that will help you with naming and recognizing your emotions. You will be able to see your experiences differently, and you'll be able to accept the existence of other frames of reference.

The therapist will be empathetic toward you, and you will be able to experience a relationship where you can just be yourself without being judged. Discovering and accepting your true self is the first step toward others wanting to know and accept you with all your strengths and weaknesses.

Empathy Exercise

- Think of a coworker who has been anxious, frustrated, irritable and grumpy.
- What do you think they are feeling?
- Try to think why they're feeling this way; are they going through something in their life? Did you contribute to them feeling this way?
- Can you feel this feeling yourself?
- Is there something you could do or say to make them feel better?

Selective Empathy

Under the topic of empathy, we also need to address selective empathy, which is undesirable. It's in our human nature to be more empathetic toward human beings who look like you, think like you, belong to the same religion, and basically have the same socio-economic background. This can pose a challenge in a workplace that consists of people from a wide variety of cultural and religious backgrounds. The challenge here is to care for individuals who are drastically different from yourself.

How can we leave the comfort of our own reality to feel empathy for a person who comes from a completely different reality than ourselves? For example, imagine you are an accountant from a privileged background whose parents could afford to send you to the best university and buy you a car, as well as pay for the best accommodation during your student years. You are used to receiving the best of everything. The people you socialized with at university are from the same background as you. However, at work, you have two colleagues from different racial and cultural backgrounds who were very underprivileged growing up. Fortunately, they are extremely intelligent and received bursaries to study. However, their parents couldn't really give them anything, and they have had to work hard for everything they have. They come from a totally different reality than you, and there might be misunderstandings between you, because of this. You need to find ways to work together.

There are a few ways in which we can challenge selective empathy, such as:

- Finding commonality. We need to be able to walk in each other's shoes and see the world beyond our own ego and pride. You need to be able to appreciate the views of your colleagues who might not come from the same privileged background as you.

- Not providing other people with solutions to problems of which you have no lived experience. This comes across as patronizing to people who have lived experience of the problems.

- Subscribing to different social media accounts and news outlets, to get more information about issues that hardly anyone pays attention to. News coverage is limited to issues that appeal to the majority.

- Standing up for others, in the workplace as well. If your colleagues suffer from inequality in your company, stand up for them. Don't budge, even if you're the only one standing up for inequality.

- There will be some who will be resistant to your changed behavior when you start standing up for others. You may feel isolated at first when you move out of your comfort zone to stand up for others. Just keep in mind that you have grown as a person, and you can only control your own growth.

The Decline in Empathy and Why Some People Are Less Empathetic

In today's society, we are experiencing a decrease in empathy and an overall increase in anger. It's an unfortunate and scary fact that people seem to care less about each other than ever before. This is a mentality that you want to change in your organization.

The environment in which people find themselves also plays a role in fostering or destroying empathy.

The decline in empathy, excessive stress, and a burnout culture that is deemed acceptable, all go hand-in-hand. People have become so conditioned that stress is the norm, as well as to the belief that they use all their energy to focus on their own survival, work, raising children, and whatever busy work they need to do. At the end of the day, most people don't really have time to consider the world around them and what is happening to other people in it. Headlines of murder and war flash across our conscious minds before we almost instantly forget about them again.

Younger people, in particular, have been exposed to a performance-oriented lifestyle since a young age. Many of them have been so focused on getting ahead, they have never had the time or opportunity to focus on improving their emotional intelligence. With full school and study schedules, they are used to being pressured to achieve since early childhood. They have never really experienced boredom either, as there has always been some form of amusement available to keep their minds occupied, such as computer games and backseat DVD players in cars.

The truth is that our modern lifestyle is making it increasingly hard to be empathetic toward each other.

The fact that a lot of communication doesn't take place in person anymore, but instead via email, text messages or social media, doesn't help either. You will find that your younger employees are hard-working and goal-oriented, but their loyalty toward their employers can be low, and they don't have much experience at being empathetic. This may make them struggle to get along with other team members.

However, it's not only the younger generations who display lower levels of empathy. Older generations, like the Baby Boomers, are increasingly displaying lower levels of empathy as they are increasingly exposed to achievement-focused stimuli.

In general, people have to work more and also face more pressure at work. Expectations and pressures are always getting higher, and they don't have as much time for people in their lives, as they used to. We have become a process-focused society that is always striving for faster turnaround times.

We could also say that electronics have created an empathy barrier between people. You are less likely to recognize people's emotions if you communicate electronically or take their needs into consideration, when you can't see them. You are more likely to say things electronically to people that you won't say to their faces.

A person's background could also play a role in why they are less empathetic.

Children learn empathy while growing up, and it could be that they didn't experience much empathy while growing up.

All of us can be selectively empathetic, if someone's experiences are just too far removed from our way of life for us to understand properly. You may find that you even feel guilty for not being able to empathize with someone else's pain.

It could be that you do feel empathetic to someone, but you are just not emotionally intelligent enough to display this behavior or use the correct language.

Empathy also tends to take a backseat in our lives if we have been experiencing stress for a long time, and we are mentally and physically exhausted. If you are too overwhelmed to cope with your life, it's unlikely that you will not feel empathy for anyone else.

Burnout could also lead to emotional detachment, as well as depression and anxiety. People with these conditions will need all their mental energy to deal with their own problems.

Some people who may suffer from personality disorders, such as borderline personality disorder, also struggle to be empathetic. They may appear indifferent in the way they react to others.

People who have been abused can be less empathetic or often more empathetic to others. People whose trust has been abused also won't be empathetic toward other people.

Key Takeaways

- Empathy is about recognizing other people's emotions and sharing their perspectives. It can help you build and strengthen relationships.
- Cognitive empathy is when you are aware on an intellectual level of the emotional state of another person.
- Emotional empathy is when you engage with and share emotions with other people.
- Compassionate empathy is when your actions support other people.
- You need to give your coworker your full attention, in order to use empathy effectively in the workplace. Consider verbal and

nonverbal clues to understand their situation. Acknowledge your colleague's feelings and take positive action that will improve their well-being.

- Selective empathy is when you are more empathetic toward human beings who look like you, think like you, and are from the same background.

- Selective empathy can be a problem in a workplace that has many employees from a wide variety of cultural and religious backgrounds. The challenge is to care about people who are drastically different from yourself.

- Empathy has decreased in modern society and we experience an exponential increase in anger.

- The environment in which people find themselves also plays a role in fostering or destroying empathy.

- Empathy is learned in childhood, but if you haven't experienced much empathy as a child, you can still learn it as an adult.

- People have fewer opportunities to experience empathy today as a result of our performance-oriented culture.

Social Awareness in the Workplace

When you are a manager, you need to be socially aware at work. You need to understand how your employees feel about the new work coming their way. If some of your employees are looking glum in a meeting where a project is being discussed, it means that not all of them are happy about the idea of being involved with it. This means they won't be able to give their best, and you need to be able to understand why.

You need to acknowledge the emotions of your employees, but don't try to change them. You don't have to agree with their feelings, but they will feel better if you let them know you notice they are struggling.

It's vital to take people's past into account when it comes to their behavior. They would have learned their behavior from their parents and family members during childhood. Certain types of behavior could also be a strategy to survive socially or fit into a certain group.

Instead of becoming frustrated by people's behavior, you need to think about the following aspects of their behavior:

- What type of needs might your employee be fulfilling through their behavior?
- What type of acknowledgment are they hoping to get through their behavior?
- What could have happened to them in the past that explains their behavior as adults?

Unresolved Childhood Trauma

Your employees could be suffering from unresolved issues from childhood. Psychologist Alice Miller says people can face significant emotional consequences for not dealing with childhood trauma. Miller has done research into the lives of dictators like Stalin and Hitler. In her series of books, she comes to the conclusion that most dictators, terrorists, and murderers suffered abuse during childhood, which they have never come to terms with. The only way they could survive is to deny the feelings of helplessness they experienced as children, and by dominating and abusing other people as adults. This denial of childhood pain made them incapable of experiencing empathy as adults.

Even people who weren't abused as children could suffer the consequences of childhood neglect or authoritarian parenting as adults. Miller says the "poisonous pedagogy" (Miller, 2015) we experience as children, can make it difficult to get in touch with our feelings during adulthood.

According to Miller, many of our behavioral and societal problems are caused by the rage and violence which are taught to children during childhood, especially those children who are brought up with corporal punishment. The children have to suppress their rage during childhood for the sake of their own survival. These tendencies tend to come back in adulthood when children, who suffered and were bullied, often become bullies themselves. It's unfortunate when these tendencies also emerge in the workplace, especially when people in leadership positions are the bullies who abuse their employees. If you recognize that you display some of these behavioral characteristics, you need to get therapy, so that you can deal with your childhood trauma. It isn't fair to everyone around you if you are always taking out your emotional frustrations on them, and it will also lead to a high staff turnover.

Part of the problem and the cause of many unresolved issues is that we were simply told we need to grow up, get over it, and move on. Many people receive these messages from childhood, to the degree where it's unacceptable to connect to their emotions.

As a result of childhood issues, many people develop false beliefs about themselves. They could believe that something is wrong with them, and that they deserve to be treated badly. They could even see themselves as bad or over-sensitive people. Adults can become stuck in their psychological development as a result of these issues.

Some of us who are adults today have grown up with the mentality that beating children is a normal part of raising them, and that it's ultimately for their own good. However, the violence that is in all levels of our society and also often found in the workplace, indicates that disempowered children will strive to regain their power as adults—mostly in toxic ways.

If you have employees who suffer from anxiety and depression, including yourself, it's a good idea to get in touch with your childhood emotions, even if they're unpleasant. This will make it easier to understand the reasons behind your actions. The suppressed emotions that are stored in our bodies could be causing a wide range of negative emotions in adulthood, including panic attacks and violent behavior.

If we become more aware of our behavior and what is causing it, we can prevent ourselves from behaving in unsuitable ways in the workplace, and we will also be less affected by the bad behavior of other people. If you report to a manager who behaves in demoralizing ways, it's important to recognize that this person probably has unresolved issues of their own. They may be verbally aggressive, but they don't have the power to beat you like your parents used to do.

Anxiety can also be a result of what someone experienced during childhood. For example, as a child, they may have lived in constant fear of the next time their toxic parent(s) would have an emotional meltdown and beat them. As an adult, these types of people are left with a constant fear that they have to avoid danger when there is no danger threatening them.

Transference

Suppressed feelings can lead to transference as adults. This is the phenomenon of transferring negative feelings we have for an authority figure, such as our parents, onto other people, such as our managers at work—or even our romantic partners, which could lead to relationship problems. It's possible to deal with this if you see it as a consequence of what you experienced during your childhood.

People who are dealing with this problem need to relive the fear they had of their parents, and view them as clearly as possible. They need to deal with their emotional baggage, realize what happened to them, and then decide to act in a different way.

It's important that we confront this period of our lives, as it has a huge impact on our adult selves.

Getting in touch with your childhood self, and reevaluating what happened to you, can have a major impact on your adult life. For one thing, it can help you understand where many health issues come from, such as anxiety, high blood pressure, stomach ulcers, or insomnia. Once you have confronted your symptoms, you will find your physical and mental health will start to improve.

People can also improve their relationships in the workplace once they realize how their current behavior is still being influenced by the relationships they had with their childhood caregivers. They should be able to stand up for themselves, be more empathetic with others, and act in less aggressive ways.

Therapy can be beneficial to people who struggle with childhood trauma, as it can help them free themselves from their fears and leave the chaos of their childhood behind. When they're finally able to be emotionally honest with themselves, they can get rid of their denial.

When you are able to confront your past through therapy, you won't want to take out your anger on surrogate victims any longer. It will free you, once you understand your anger is a result of not being understood and accepted when you were a child. Once you are able to experience your unexpressed emotions, you will learn how to know yourself better.

The Importance of Social Intelligence at Work

Social intelligence is required for effective management, and for teams to work well together. SQ can be closely linked to emotional intelligence (EQ), and is basically the extension of EQ's relationship management competency. It is your ability to manage your emotional skills, which are needed to read social situations and then react to them in a socially acceptable way, which will get other people to work together and co-exist.

If managers and employees have SQ skills, it can have the following benefits for the company:

- It will be easier to get along with peers. If everyone has a better working relationship, it becomes easier for them to work together toward the same goal.
- Individuals will understand the effects of their actions on teams. Team members will feel they're adding value, and it will be easier for them to align with team goals.
- If you have a culturally diverse workforce, it's important to note that people will react differently to situations according to their cultural backgrounds and upbringing. Culture days or intercultural training can help employees understand why their colleagues may act differently in certain situations. This will make it easier for employees to develop respect for each other.
- Social-emotional intelligence can help you make progress in your career. People who lack this skill are often overlooked for promotions. People in a workforce need to be able to work together to achieve a common goal. It's essential to learn social intelligence skills to understand other people's nonverbal behavior and emotions so that we can relate to them better.

As a manager, you need to be socially aware and able to read a room.

You can become more socially aware in some of the following ways:

- Learn how to empathize. We have become so used to competition and deadlines at work, that we have stopped caring about the feelings of our colleagues and teammates. If you can't tell when a colleague is emotionally stressed, you lack social awareness.

- You can practice how to be more empathetic to your team. If someone has made a mistake, don't go off at them, but try to determine why it happened. Maybe they were stressing out about something, or they are experiencing stress in their personal lives. Empathy can really help you as a manager, as it will assist you in getting the best out of your employees.
- You need to learn to listen before you speak. The constant stress of having to get things done in the corporate world has led to people speaking more, but listening less.
- The reality is that nobody enjoys working with a bossy manager who places orders and never listens to their employees' opinions. Teams fall apart if you have managers who aren't socially aware and don't understand basic human emotions.
- It's essential that you create an environment where people feel safe in sharing their feelings.

Key Takeaways

- When you are a manager, you need to be socially aware at work. You need to understand how your employees feel about the new work coming their way.

- It's important to understand that the behavior of some of your employees, including you, can be influenced by childhood trauma.
- The denial of childhood pain can make it almost impossible for people to express empathy for others.
- Suppressed feelings can lead to transference as adults. This is the phenomenon of transferring negative feelings we have for an authority figure, such as our parents, onto other people, such as our managers at work.

- Social intelligence is required for effective management and for teams to work well together. SQ can be closely linked to emotional intelligence (EQ).

- Social-emotional intelligence can help you make progress in your career.

Respectful Feedback

As a manager, you need to be able to give clear, respectful, and warm feedback. It's important to give feedback consistently. Your feedback should also be behavior-specific. The feedback should always focus on the behavior and not the person.

It's acceptable to praise your employees in public, but deliver criticism behind closed doors. Always make your expectations clear, and provide them with constructive feedback. Mentoring can also be useful.

Giving Effective Feedback

Employees need feedback to improve. Most employees rely on feedback from their managers in order to know where to improve. However, many managers are uncomfortable when it comes to giving feedback, and may do it in such a vague way that it's difficult to understand.

If employees don't receive sufficient feedback, they will struggle to improve their performance.

For example, if you tell someone they did a great job, it will make them feel good about themselves and their performance, but they won't be sure how to do it the next time they have to.

You have to tell them in more detail what was good about their performance so that they will know how to replicate it. For example, tell them that the document they produced was on time, that it didn't contain any errors, and that the cover design was innovative and contributed to the company's positive image.

Model for Effective Feedback

Effective feedback should be specific, functional, and concrete. You can set your feedback out in the following way:

- Set the context for your feedback. Everyone needs to be focused on the same issue and this is also the opportunity for you to be specific. You can comment on the behavior you observed, and not on someone's personality or character. When giving your feedback, you need to be able to answer when something occurred, where you were at the time, and who was involved.

- From there, you need to state what you observed. What did you see? This will probably be the most difficult part of giving feedback. People are good at creating stories, which might mean we can jump to conclusions and assign blame without first considering other information and interpretations. Always focus on behavior, as that can be changed. For example, if someone was screaming and yelling at another employee, describe their actions to them instead of telling them that they were being a jerk.

- Explain to someone how their behavior makes you feel, but be careful how you go about it. You can let them know what you thought about their performance, but also what reactions you may have observed in others. For example, if your employee pauses too long after speaking, you can tell them that clients seemed to lose interest and looked away from him.

- When you provide the feedback, you also need to think about the following:

What was the impact of the behavior on the business?

What was the effect of the behavior on you, and how did you feel?

- Reaffirm your expectations when you give feedback. Tell your employees what you expect from them. Would it be the same behavior, or do you want them to improve on their behavior? This will help your employees understand what is expected of them to be successful. However, it's important not to give vague feedback. For example, don't tell the employee that they need to be better prepared. Instead, tell them to make sure that they can respond faster, and that there are shorter pauses between the questions and answers. This could lead to a conversation about how to prepare better in the future.

- If you feel you struggle to get the right message across, you can also write down what you want to say. Try to get your thoughts in order by writing notes that you can keep with you during the meeting so that you can refer to whatever you want to highlight.

- Be prepared that during the conversation some employees can become defensive about their performance if you tell them what they could have done better. Just keep stirring the conversation in a constructive direction, as this could help you sort out a lot of employee issues.

- Respect should be an important part of the conversation. You need to make sure the conversation is based on mutual respect and understanding. This is essential, as you don't want there to be hard feelings after the conversation. Employees need to feel valued, even after you have to give them direction.

- Take an approach that you need to work together on to fix problems. If you give them some information that might not be that easy to hear, also look at finding solutions. Commit yourself to working together with the employee to fix the problem in both the short and long-term.
- After the initial feedback, you need to follow up with your employees on a regular basis, so that everything is going as planned.

Where Can Feedback Go Wrong?

There are many reasons that an innocent feedback session can go wrong. Maybe both the manager and employee are too emotional and the focus is too personal, instead of the focus being on the employee's behavior.

Since our brains have evolved to protect us from perceived harm, we might fight back against feedback, if we perceive that it might do us harm.

Negative feedback can threaten our self-esteem, but also our need for safety and security, as we might feel as if we could lose our job.

Your tone and how you deliver the feedback as a manager will also determine how it's received. You should take care that your criticism is not destructive, by using a harsh tone that could imply the poor performance is a result of the personal characteristics that can't be changed.

Also beware that you might not be delivering feedback that is superficially polite, but actually implies that the recipient is unworthy.

Key Takeaways

- Managers need to give clear and respectful feedback.
- Feedback needs to be consistent and behavior-specific.
- While you can praise your employees in public, only deliver criticism behind closed doors. Make sure your feedback is constructive.

Individualize Your Approach

Once you have the approaches and strategies you are going to use, you need to adjust them so that they can fit the individuals you have in your organization. Also, make sure the strategies you use suit your personal style of leadership. This could be something simple, such as adjusting your tone of voice or the setting when you give feedback to different employees.

The modern workforce has a growing problem with increasing turnover, and employees who aren't engaged, which is a serious threat to the profitability and productivity of your company.

Helping employees get engaged and see the value of their jobs and the vision of the company, will take commitment from the leadership of the company.

Functional Attitude Theory

The Functional attitude theory looks at ways of increasing employee engagement. According to this theory, if a persuasive message agrees with a person's needs and attitudes regarding a topic, the person will respond favorably to it.

The theory states there are five basic functional attitudes. If you recognize how they appear in your organization and how you can attend to them, this will help you increase employee engagement in your business.

- Instrumental or utilitarian function. These types of employees want to get the best type of understanding, which will help them do their jobs as well as possible. They'll want the right equipment and training to do their jobs. Make sure that the correct office supplies, software, and training are available to these people.

- Social-adjustive. These employees either want to nurture relationships with others they look up to, or they want to emphasize how different they are from undesirable others. Some of these employees may become disengaged when they feel they don't get enough opportunity to interact with others, or they could feel they're not getting enough recognition for the work they are doing.

  The productivity of these employees may actually increase with social interaction, and recognition and performance management can get them excited about their work. You can get these employees engaged by holding team standup meetings, giving regular feedback, and recognizing their contributions.

- Value-expressive. These employees look for value in their work, and they also enjoy working on projects that support their core values and beliefs. Their desire is to improve the lives of others, and support something they believe in, such as supporting the environment. These employees may become disengaged if they don't see the outcome of the work they are doing. Make them aware of the customers' lives that are being improved by your company's product. They will also be motivated if you tell them you value and respect them, and you let them leave work early to look after their children's needs.

- Ego-defensive. People develop this attitude when they want to protect their self-esteem, and they want to reduce feelings of being threatened. These employees value their education and skills, and they are proud of who they are and what they can do. They will lose interest in their job if they haven't got enough responsibility, and they weren't trusted or respected enough. It's essential to give them the recognition they need. If you recognize the contributions and accomplishments of these employees, they will become engaged in the work.
- Knowledge. Employees with this attitude want to organize the world. They want to know what it takes to do their jobs well. These employees will be very dedicated if you give them experienced mentors, training, and dedication.

Individualization

Individualization demonstrates that a business cares about its employees. It gives modern employees room for personal development and freedom, while it helps workers produce in ways they find the most rewarding.

You can use some of the individualization strategies to show your employees that your business cares about them, and is willing to make sacrifices for them.

Allow them to work remotely, when they need it, even if it's on a regular basis. Working remotely has become almost a norm since the COVID-19 pandemic, even though many companies have asked their employees to return to the office once COVID regulations were lifted. It has now been proven that working from home actually increases the productivity of many workers, and also leads to higher satisfaction among workers. This is especially useful for working mothers, who often have to organize their children's activities as well.

Working remotely also ensures that workers have more cash in their pockets at the end of the month, with fuel prices skyrocketing around the globe.

If working from home is not an option, give your employees flexible working time. Strict 9 to 5 working schedules (or much later for many people) have started becoming obsolete, even before the pandemic. Communication technologies are so developed that it's become easier to work from home, and if you're on a flexible schedule, you can miss peak hour traffic. You don't have to make this an everyday thing, but short days with flexibility can motivate your employees and could be a valuable benefit for many people.

Reconsider the contracts you have with your employees. Consider allowing them the ability to look for contract and freelance work outside of your organization. This can help them achieve certain goals, without requiring them to resign from your company.

Help your employees develop themselves, their skills, and their own personal brand. This will show that you are invested in your employees and you don't just regard them as cogs in a machine. They'll tend to stay longer if you treat them well and give them greater flexibility.

Reshape and change the roles on your team. It's a good idea to keep the roles and positions fluid when you hire new staff. Change the responsibilities for the roles if you think this is necessary, or write new job descriptions. If you can use your employees' strengths, your company will achieve more and your team will also work better together.

Key Takeaways

- The functional attitude theory looks at ways of increasing employee engagement. According to this theory, if a persuasive message agrees with a person's needs and attitudes regarding a topic, the person will respond favorably to it.

- According to the FA theory, there are five basic functional attitudes. They can help you increase employee engagement if you recognize how they appear in your organization.

Staying Motivated and Keeping Your Employees Motivated

Emotionally intelligent managers and employees will find it easier to stay motivated at work when circumstances are difficult. Everything doesn't always go according to plan, and even large companies can lose clients and have to downsize.

Over the last few years, the business environment hasn't been easy due to the COVID-19 pandemic, and geopolitical upheaval around the globe has made the situation even more complex.

One of the first positive steps you need to take is to accept that the situation is temporary.

Maybe it feels as if you and your employees are swamped with work, and expectations are increasing every day. However, as a result of budget cuts, you are unable to appoint more staff. If you assign too much work to your employees, it will just decrease their morale. Instead, you can choose to focus on quick wins.

The quick wins will keep your employees going when they are faced with a large amount of work to complete. Small wins will motivate employees as they let the brain know that you're making progress and that success could be imminent.

Good managers will also highlight all the successes that are achieved during difficult times. You're giving employees hope that the hard time is almost over, and that things will change for the better. If you have a positive mindset, you can also see challenges as positive opportunities to make changes in your organization.

It's an opportunity to introduce new energy and use the crisis to make your company more competitive.

Emotionally intelligent leaders will set goals that are manageable, but not easily achievable. They won't be deterred by negativity when it comes to reaching their goals.

Emotionally intelligent leaders also adapt well to change and will adjust their values with time. They are also flexible, but will remain focused on their goals and plans.

A leader with high EI is committed to their company and this keeps them focused, even when they're not motivated. This type of manager will consider progress, how their team can improve, and how far they are from reaching their goals.

Key Takeaways

- Emotionally intelligent people find it easier to stay motivated at work when circumstances are difficult.

- Quick wins will keep your employees motivated when they have a lot of work to complete.

Chapter 4:

A Blueprint for a Psychologically Safe Organization

If we want to decrease staff turnover in our organizations, we need to ensure that our employees feel happy, valued, and effective at work. To do this, we need to create an organization that is characterized by a high degree of psychological safety, which is supported by the emotional intelligence of all its employees.

A safe platform for providing and seeking feedback, and speaking up against bad behavior and all forms of discrimination, where employees are free to share their thoughts and emotions, will greatly support this goal.

Creating a Culture of Sharing Thoughts and Emotions

If your employees are satisfied and fulfilled, you can grow your bottom line. This is the approach Google has followed, and it has worked exceptionally well for them.

Google Company Culture

Google has tried to create opportunities for its employees to come together in innovative ways. The different channels employees can use include:

- The Google Cafés platform encourages interaction between and within teams, about work and also more social aspects. Google employees also have the option of sending emails directly to the company's leaders.

- The innovative Google Moderator was designed by Google's engineers. The idea is that when people have meetings, anyone can ask a question, and the participants can then vote on the questions they want to have answered.

  Moderator is one of Google's 20 percent projects. Google allows its engineers to spend 20% of their week working on projects that interest them, which allows the company to benefit more from their different talents.

- Google has weekly TGIF meetings where employees can ask the company's top leaders questions about company issues.

- Google Universal Ticketing Systems (GUTS) is a way that issues can be filed about anything, and then reviewed for problems or patterns.

- FixIts are 24-hour sprints where Google staff stop anything else they're doing, and focus all their energy on focusing on specific problems.

- Employees are also asked to survey their managers, and the company uses this information to recognize the best managers. They then use these managers to mentor staff, acting as role models. Managers who have been identified as not doing well, receive coaching that helps most of them improve within a quarter.

The leadership at Google believes people are looking for meaning in their work, and they've managed to create a passionate and creative workforce.

Google also offers its employees benefits that show them they are invested in their health and well-being. They are one of the first companies that have a clear vision of understanding the needs of their employees. They also give employees the flexibility to work in ways they find the most suitable.

Some of the benefits they provide include the following:

- Free organic meals that are prepared by a chef
- Unlimited, free dry cleaning
- Game stations that include football, video games, and ping pong
- Free health and dental checkups
- Physicians that are onsite
- Gym memberships
- Free haircuts
- Car subsidies
- Death benefits to the families of deceased employees
- In-house pods to take naps

The Characteristics of Google's Organizational Characters

Google's culture is focused on innovation and improving employee performance. The aim is to effectively motivate employees through the organizational culture. The importance of the openness of employees is also emphasized with the aim of promoting innovative views.

Google's corporate culture is defined by openness, innovation, excellence, a hands-on approach, and small company family rapport.

Openness: The cultural characteristic of openness refers to the way information is shared among employees. The objective of promoting openness is to encourage the spread of valuable knowledge that can lead to further innovation. An example of this is that individual employees are motivated to interact with each other during different times of the day, as a way of improving the knowledge they use for their jobs. Google's workplace layout also encourages this interaction.

Innovation: The company's organizational culture motivates employees to contribute to the innovation of the business. The level of innovation also changes according to the needs identified in the services and information technology market.

Excellence: The cultural characteristic of excellence focuses on achieving excellence in all areas of the business. This characteristic is also incorporated into the human resources program to make sure that employees appreciate the culture of excellence. The aim of the company's training programs is to motivate employees to keep working toward improving their work and not to be happy with mediocre results. Google's push for smartness in the workforce also pushes its employees to strive for excellence.

A Hands-On Approach: Google's corporate culture also allows it to follow a hands-on approach when it comes to human resource development. Experiential learning is used to increase the skills, abilities, and knowledge of the staff. Theoretical knowledge is not enough to grow your career at Google. Employees are expected to continue learning as they continue on their journey through the company.

Small Company Family Rapport: This part of Google culture focuses on the social interaction among workers. The work environment is warm and employees feel comfortable talking and sharing ideas. The idea behind encouraging warm social relations is that it will make employees more satisfied in their jobs.

Google can be regarded as an example of effective organizational design and human resource development in the corporate culture. However, Google's organizational culture can be further improved by making information sharing even more open. While the company supports information sharing, this still happens in a controlled way.

How to Create a Culture of Knowledge Sharing at Work

A culture of knowledge sharing can take your business to the next level, but unfortunately, you get people who like to hold onto information for themselves and use it only for their benefit. This knowledge hoarding can be bad for a company's performance, as well as work relationships. Where knowledge hoarding is at the order of the day, employees are usually less satisfied, productivity is low, and organizational knowledge can be lost.

Employees also have ways of making it seem like they are sharing information, when in reality, they are keeping things close to their chest. They might tell other employees that they will share information with them but they never do, as they are too "busy." They are hoping that you will forget or give up asking them for information.

Some could also pretend they don't have the information you need, or they might tell you they are not allowed to share information, when this is simply untrue, and they could actually share it.

People who hide knowledge at work inspire other people to also hide knowledge. Where employees freely share knowledge and information, this helps them build rapport and gives them a sense of belonging, makes them feel competent, and improves the outcomes for the entire company.

Work overload and fierce competition between employees can prevent knowledge from being shared. This is especially a problem in teams where trust and empathy can be lacking between colleagues. People are also more inclined to hide their knowledge when they perceive that their colleagues need their input in their jobs (task interdependence). People are motivated to share knowledge when the autonomy and cognitive demands of their jobs increase their feeling of doing meaningful work. When people feel they're working to get approval from others, they're more inclined to hide their knowledge.

You can create a culture in your workplace where your employees are more inclined to share information, as well as their thoughts and emotions.

Don't overload people with work, as this creates time pressure. Give them stimulating work that provides them with autonomy. Make sure there are not too many dependencies between workers, as this can also create time pressures.

Do your best to create a cooperative culture in your company. Don't create competition by publically labeling people as winners or losers.

As a leader, you should also act as a role model, and share your knowledge with others. Also, show that you trust others to use the knowledge you share with them in a good way.

When you want to implement a knowledge-sharing mentality in your company, you first need to understand how everyone relates to information. Are your teams open to sharing information, or do they tend to keep everything to themselves? Is there a lot of politics that keep information away from certain people?

The ideal situation is when teams divulge their wins and failures, and share data from research freely. When the company is transparent about the good and bad results of campaigns, everyone can learn from the knowledge that teams are gathering.

One way of getting people to share knowledge, as well as to develop more rapport between them, is to consider if your meetings can be changed to place a greater focus on human connection.

See how you can change meetings in your organization or company in order to improve openness, connection, and sharing between your employees. Try to start your meetings with casual conversations, and not by jumping straight into the formal work requirements. Ask people what they did for the weekend, or what restaurants they visited.

Practices like this will make it easier for team members to work together, as they will be more comfortable if they see the personal side of their colleagues. An icebreaker at the beginning of your meeting can help people relax before you start with the real hard work.

Your office space can also be rearranged to encourage employees to share more about themselves and also the work they're doing. If your office space is cramped and closed off, it may impact your employees' ability to connect and share in a meaningful way.

When you design or redesign your office space, it's a good idea to keep openness in mind. This will enable employees to have meetings in shared spaces and learn from each other. They could engage in casual conversations with people they might not normally talk to, and learn from them in the process.

Create an Open and Sharing Culture in Your Office

Create an atmosphere of trust through an open-door policy. Employees should feel that they are free to ask other employees, and even management, for information at any time, without being judged.

- Requests for information should be seen as opportunities to connect with other employees and educate them. When the person who is asking the questions is supported, they are more likely to share their knowledge when they get the opportunity to do so.
- If you find it difficult to share content with your team and you're always looking for lost information, it might help you to install a knowledge-sharing platform. If you can find a cloud-based platform, it will improve the culture of sharing in your office and keep all the files, folders, and even emails organized.

It makes it easier to collaborate with your team members, even when they should be working remotely.

Technical tools to get the job done are becoming more popular than ever, especially since remote working has really taken off since the COVID-19 pandemic. The right software can help companies share knowledge, and employees can socialize online.

Slack is perfect for quick back-and-forth discussions, as well as knowledge sharing. Slack has organized spaces called channels, and you can have a different one for different projects and people you are liaising with.

- You will need to model knowledge sharing to your employees, by sharing content regularly with them. If your employees see you doing it, they will be more likely to embrace the idea of collaboration and sharing knowledge.
- Reward your employees who participate in knowledge sharing. It doesn't come naturally to everyone, and some people might need incentives to share their ideas with others.
- Do you feel that your new employees are often nervous to share their knowledge or show their full potential? A mentor that new employees can go to at any time with their questions might help new employees to settle down. The mentor shouldn't be their supervisor because they might be afraid of being judged while they're trying to settle down. The mentor can help the new employee speak their mind, starting from their first days at the company onward.

Another way to get new employees involved in the business quickly is to let them shadow other employees. Get them to shadow experienced employees who are willing to collaborate and share their knowledge with the newcomers. The new employees will also be more likely to feel comfortable sharing their opinions if they see experienced employees doing this. You can also ask new employees for input directly until they start feeling more confident about starting to give it out on their own.

You are going to have to be patient with your employees while you are busy creating an open culture of sharing for your business. Some of them might come from more aggressive environments where competition was valued more than working together. They might need to do a lot of adjustments to how they view colleagues working together.

Key Takeaways

- Google promotes an open company culture of sharing thoughts, feelings, and ideas. This is supported by weekly TGIF meetings where employees can ask the top leaders questions about company issues.
- Google employees are also asked to rate their managers. Managers who perform well are often asked to mentor staff.
- The leadership at Google believes people are looking for meaning in their work, and they've managed to create a passionate and creative workforce.
- Google's corporate culture is defined by openness, innovation, excellence, a hands-on approach, and small company family rapport.
- A culture of knowledge-sharing can take your business to the next level.

Taking Responsibility for Employee Interaction

If an employee who is experiencing problems, whether they be work-related or in their private life, doesn't bring this to your attention, you will need to ask yourself why this is the case.

Do some introspection and decide if it might be your body language, attitude, or voice that might have prevented the employee from asking for your help. Could you have intimidated the employee in some way, even if this wasn't your intention?

Edmonson's Matrix

Dr. Amy Edmondson, Novartis Professor of Leadership and Management at Harvard Business School, defines psychological safety as the belief that you will not be punished for speaking up with your questions, concerns, mistakes, or ideas (Edmonson, 1999).

According to Dr. Edmondson, management needs to do three things to promote psychological safety in the workplace. If there is an issue with work, it should be seen as a learning problem and not an execution problem. You have hired the person because they have the right experience and qualifications for the job. If the person delivers work that is in some way not satisfactory, it might be that they just need more training and feedback in specific aspects of the job.

Dr. Edmonson believes it will also promote psychological safety in your work environment if managers acknowledge their own fallibility and model curiosity. If you do this, it will make your employees feel safer to speak up and admit their own mistakes.

With Edmondson's approach, the leader becomes part of the team. The leader doesn't know all the answers and needs the team's input.

Dr. Edmondson also addresses management's fear that psychological safety will lessen the emphasis on accountability for results. She created a 2x2 matrix with psychological safety on the y-axis and accountability on the x-axis.

The matrix is divided as follows:

- Apathy zone (low psychological safety and low accountability)
- Comfort zone (high psychological safety and low accountability)
- Anxiety zone (low psychological safety and high accountability)
- Learning zone (high psychological safety and high accountability).

Many organizations operate in the anxiety zone of the Edmondson matrix, and people are scared to speak up as they don't want to be ridiculed. This zone is bad for innovation and will have a negative impact on the growth of the company.

The aim is to get your company in the learning zone, where people feel both accountable and psychologically safe. This will only be achieved if management manages to create an environment where questions can be asked and mistakes mentioned, without fear of reprisal. People need to learn to work together in the modern working world, and that competitiveness won't get them any rewards.

Psychological safety in an organization doesn't mean the company's performance will suffer, but rather, it will improve. There could be an adjustment period at first when it comes to reporting errors and problems. It's vital that managers don't overreact if errors appear to increase at first when people feel safe to report them. This situation should stabilize as employees learn from each other's errors going forward.

Key Takeaways

- Dr. Amy Edmondson, Novartis Professor of Leadership and Management at Harvard Business School, created a matrix with four zones in which businesses find themselves; namely an apathy zone, comfort zone, anxiety zone, and learning zone.

- Many organizations operate in the anxiety zone of the matrix, as employees are scared to speak up because they fear they will be ridiculed.

Open-Door Policy and One-on-One Meetings

Another way to encourage employee interaction is to have an open-door policy at times that work for you. Let your employees know when your door is open to them and that, as their leader, you're asking them to come to your office to talk about whatever they need to bring to your attention. You can also tell people to look in your web calendar to see when you are available.

You can also proactively seek out your employees and ask them about their well-being. Some employees won't offer to share their thoughts and feelings if they have to seek you out, but might feel safer if you ask them.

One-on-One Meetings

Having regular one-on-one meetings with your employees can help you find out if there are any problems in the team, and help you diffuse difficult situations before they get worse.

For example, Ben meets with his employees once every two weeks. From the different conversations, he can piece together that there is tension between different team members. This information helps him manage the situation in one-on-one sessions with the various employees before the situation gets out of control.

Tom is extremely busy and he can think of better ways of spending his time than having one-on-one sessions with his employees. He keeps canceling sessions, as he sees them as a waste of time. After a few months, Tom becomes aware of declining productivity in the team. It seems colleagues are fighting, and some of them can't work together at all. There are rumors about people, and the situation is getting out of control. No one could address any of the matters with Tom, since he was never available to speak to anyone about challenges they were experiencing.

This is why you need to use these meetings with your employees to empower yourself and the organization.

Regular meetings with your team members can also help you in other ways.

The Benefits of One-on-One Meetings

One of the main benefits is that these meetings can improve your team's productivity and the quality of their work. Employees who meet regularly with their managers are also more engaged with their work than those who don't get this opportunity.

Healthy communication between an employee and their manager is very important. One-on-ones can take a lot of time if you have many people reporting to you, but it's worth the time investment.

They give you and your employees the opportunity to discuss ideas, priorities, and how to remove obstacles that might be preventing the employee from performing at an optimal level.

These meetings are also essential for effective delegation to your employees. The one-on-ones will also help managers save time, as all the questions will come to you at once, during the meeting, and people won't come to you with many small questions during the week.

The meetings can also help managers build honest relationships, and help you interact in a positive way with your team. You can show that you care personally about them, and that you are invested in their growth.

You may feel somewhat awkward expressing your appreciation to employees, but this is also a good way to build trust.

Also, make sure that you record your one-on-one meetings or make notes of what was said. You will show your employees that you care about their concerns if you can remember what was said during previous meetings.

One-on-ones create the perfect environment for the exchange of feedback between management and employees. It's the ideal opportunity to discuss issues you won't want to discuss in big meetings where your other colleagues are present. Don't waste time discussing topics that can be discussed in regular meetings.

Key Takeaways

- If you have one-on-one meetings with your employees, you can sort out our problems before they get worse.

- One-on-one meetings can help managers and employees build healthy relationships.
- Managers can also seek out employees and ask them about their well-being. Some employees won't offer to share their thoughts and feelings, but will do so if managers ask them about themselves.

Effective Strategies for Sharing Thoughts and Emotions

Psychological safety should become a mantra and an integral part of your company's culture. It will only benefit your organization in the long run.

Professor Edmondson pinpointed certain benefits for companies such as a constant improvement of quality, increased productivity, and a culture of lifelong learning. Psychologically safe teams are also better when it comes to innovating and adapting to change.

Edmonson's work shows that fear is still used as a motivational instrument in hierarchical systems. However, research has shown that fear makes you more unproductive, as it takes cognitive resources away from the parts of your brain that process new information. If employees are always working in fear, they will struggle to come up with new ideas, as well as think analytically. Their productivity will also be affected as well as the quality of the final product.

Employees also need the opportunity to share their emotions in a safe way. Innovation and creativity are some of the benefits of sharing emotions at work.

The first thing you need to do when it comes to sharing thoughts and emotions is to stop dismissing your employees' emotions.

Employees are often expected not to display any emotion at work, as it's considered unprofessional. However, new research has shown that it's actually beneficial for teams to share their emotions and respond empathetically to each other, as this can increase their problem-solving ability and will improve idea generation.

As the manager, you need to create an environment in which your team members feel safe to communicate. Your employees may be reluctant to communicate about more sensitive issues such as emotions and conflicts. You need to set things up so that your team won't feel self-conscious to speak about emotions, concerns, and even any grievances they may have.

Strategies for Encouraging Employees to Share Thoughts and Emotions

There are some useful strategies you can implement to encourage your employees to speak out, including:

- Make a point of going through your department with a list of questions, asking for feedback on specific issues. The nature of the questions should be about what is going well and what could be improved. Listen closely to the responses you receive, as this could give you themes that the employees can report back on together, with actions that were taken to improve the situation.

- You need to prove to your employees that it's worthwhile to speak out. You need to prove to them that what they say is valuable to you, as speaking up takes courage, and can be used to create positive change in your work environment and build stronger relationships. Your team members will also share more if they see that you take their concerns seriously.

- Create a culture of actively seeking feedback in your business. When there is a feeling of safety, your team members will be more likely to give feedback.

- If your staff members share their emotions with you about anything that happened in the workplace or any other concerns they may have, don't make them feel like they're in the wrong. Don't argue with them about any feedback, but thank them for their input. Also, invite them to come up with solutions to problems. For example, if there are some employees who don't get along, what do they suggest could help them get along?

- Listen to what your employees tell you without passing judgment on them. They will open up more about what is on their minds when they feel you are genuinely interested in what they have to say.

- Don't just accept obvious superficial answers, for example when somebody tells you they are doing well, but you can clearly see that all is not well. Assure people that it's safe to be open and to provide truthful answers. You can do this by asking questions such as, "Can you tell me what is wrong?" and "Would you tell me if you weren't doing well?" This will also encourage your employees to share more.

- Work toward creating a trusting relationship with your employees. They will be more inclined to share their emotions, thoughts, concerns, and ideas when they trust their leadership. If you want a strong relationship with your employees, trust is the foundation. When you show that you take their feedback to heart, employees will also be more inclined to trust you.

- The work environment should also be meaningful, in order to encourage employees to be more vocal about their concerns, emotions, and ideas.

- You also need to lead by example to create a workplace where your employees will feel comfortable sharing. Set the example by voicing concerns and other honest feedback to your team members. You need to demonstrate that everyone's opinions are valued.

- If you receive complaints that may seem unfounded, it can be difficult to deal with them. However, if you investigate these complaints, you can get potentially valuable information about the operations in your business. That is why it's important to ask questions and suggestions for improvement.

Conflict Management in the Workplace

Have you experienced conflict in your team? Are there always people who can't seem to get along? This is a normal part of day-to-day life. However, if the conflict is not managed, it can lead to frustration, anger, and pain. In our modern work environment, people are often from different cultural backgrounds and their viewpoints may be vastly different.

Where people have very different outlooks and views about challenges, disagreements are inevitable.

Conflicts can't always be prevented, but the goal should be to resolve them in an efficient manner. It's vital to establish processes to manage conflict in your company, as it will help reduce conflict among the employees.

It doesn't have to be difficult to manage conflict if you follow these steps:

- First of all, you need to determine the source of the conflict. If you can find the cause, you can begin to understand how the conflict got out of control. You will have to discuss the issues and needs that are not being met, with both parties who are involved in the conflict. Obtain as much information as possible and keep asking questions until you're sure everyone involved understands the issue.

- Find a private place to discuss the problem peacefully. Try to discuss the problems in a constructive way and give each party involved in the disagreement enough time to voice their views.

- The approach of the meeting must be positive and assertive. Set some rules for the meeting if it seems that this will be necessary. If you take this approach it will encourage people to be open and honest, and everyone will be able to understand the reasons for the conflict, as well as be able to identify solutions.

- After you receive all the information and concerns from the different parties, take your time to investigate the case. Don't just come up with a verdict based on what you've heard. Make sure you get some more information first on what happened and the parties involved. You need to have conversations with everyone who was involved and listen carefully to make sure you understand their viewpoints. Also, you need to investigate if there are any underlying sources of conflict.

- When managing conflict, the aim should be to solve the issue, as well as make sure it doesn't occur again. Brainstorm ideas with the different parties involved in the conflict on how the same issue can be prevented in the future.

- Decide on the best solution to the problem, and determine the responsibilities of the different parties in the resolution. After determining ways through which the issue can be solved, the different parties need to agree on the best solutions.

- Evaluate the resolution process and decide on preventative strategies that can be used in the future. Keep an eye on the situation to determine if the solution is effective. Take action if the issue should resurface.

The Thomas-Kilmann Model

If conflict at work isn't resolved, it can become worse with time and affect the team's morale, relationships, and productivity.

The Thomas-Kilmann model was developed in the 1970s by the researchers Kenneth Thomas and Ralph Kilmann. The model refers to 'conflict' as a condition in which people can't align their concerns with each other. If different people or groups care about contradictory things, they're going to get into conflict.

The model has two core dimensions for conflict situations, namely 'assertiveness' and 'cooperativeness.' Assertiveness describes the extent to which you try to solve the problem to your preferred outcome. Cooperativeness can be seen as the level to which you try to solve the other party's problems.

The Thomas-Kilmann model has five models for handling conflict:

1.   Competing

This approach is assertive and non-cooperative. Here you will only address your own concerns and ignore the other party's concerns.

This mode is focused on power and the aim is to get a favorable outcome for oneself. The individual's financial power and position in the hierarchy will matter the most. It's all about trying to win and standing up for yourself.

Competing is also known as forcing. The individual pursues their own concerns and pushes their viewpoint and remains resistant to other people's actions. This can be effective in certain situations, for example where less forceful methods haven't worked. It can also be used in situations where you have to stand up for yourself and resist aggression, or where a quick resolution is needed, for example in the case of a potentially life-threatening situation.

Be careful how you use forcing, as it may affect your relationship with the other person. It may also encourage your opponent to respond forcefully even if they weren't planning on responding in this way originally.

This approach may be exhausting to many people.

2. Accommodating

This mode is accepting and cooperative. The individual involved is accommodating and will listen to the problems of the other party involved in the argument. There is an element of self-sacrifice involved that can include generosity and understanding. Accommodating could also mean that you might be required to follow another person's orders when you wouldn't like to do so, or submit to other people's decisions or perspectives.

Accommodating is also known as smoothing. Here you would accommodate the concerns of other people first.

Smoothing is appropriate in the following cases:

- The issue is more important to the other person. You actually don't care about it that much.
- You can get temporary relief from the conflict until you're in a better position to respond.
- You accept you're wrong and continued conflict seems detrimental.

Another advantage of smoothing is that it provides an opportunity to assess a situation from a different angle. Just be aware that your opponent may try to take advantage of your tendency to be accommodating. You need to maintain the right balance between being accommodating and being assertive. Your confidence in responding to an opponent may be affected.

3. Avoiding

Avoiding is unassertive and uncooperative. The person doesn't want to address their own problems, nor the problems of other people. They often don't want to engage in conflict and choose to ignore the issue. They could also put off dealing with the issue or completely step away from it.

Avoiding is also known as withdrawing. It might be appropriate to withdraw in certain situations, such as where an issue is not worth the effort, and where you have more important issues to attend to and don't really have time to deal with it. Postponing is also appropriate when you see there is going to be a lot of hostility and you'll be unable to deal with the conflict.

Withdrawing can be beneficial, as it's a low-stress approach and gives you the opportunity to focus on more important issues. You also have more time to collect information before you react.

The danger of withdrawing is that it can weaken your position as a manager. Inaction can also be interpreted as agreement and your relationship with the party in the disagreement that is expecting you to take action can be affected.

4. Collaborating

This option will benefit all parties and is assertive and cooperative. It is the opposite of avoiding. The parties will work together to find a solution to the problem.

The parties need to work together to understand why there is a disagreement. It also involves looking at creative answers for interpersonal issues.

Collaborating is also known as a win-win situation. This involves working with the other party to find a solution to the problem that strives to satisfy both parties as much as possible. Collaborating can be appropriate when the commitment of the other parties is important, and a long-term relationship is important. The advantages of collaborating is that it reinforces respect and mutual trust, and the parties all share responsibility for the outcome.

This method could require more time and effort than the other methods so it may not be practical when you have too little time.

5. Compromising

The goal is to find a solution that satisfies both parties. This falls in the middle between competing and accommodating. It addresses an issue more directly, but the investigation process is not as thorough as the collaborating outcome. Compromising could also involve looking for a middle ground.

Compromising is also known as reconciling. This approach looks for a solution that satisfies both parties.

This approach is appropriate when goals are moderately important and it's not worthwhile to use forcing or collaborating. It can also be used for temporary settlement of complicated issues, as well as when the parties involved don't know each other well and haven't developed much trust. On top of this, it can be used where collaborating or forcing don't work.

Compromise can be used when issues need to be resolved and when there is not enough time. Compromise can also lower tension and stress as a result of conflict.

Avoiding Conflict

Even though conflict in the workplace isn't always a bad thing, it could also lead to ongoing problems among employees. As a manager, it's better to prevent conflict if it's possible.

Conflict in the workplace usually occurs when employees are strongly opposed to each other's ideas, and they're not willing to compromise. Conflict can result in a lot of uncomfortable tension, arguments, and abusive relationships.

When you realize you might find yourself in a nasty conflict, don't react. Rather, choose to walk away if you see the other person involved in the conflict is unable to listen to you. However, if you feel you might end up saying things that are better left unsaid, the best option is to walk away before you do damage to your reputation as a leader.

Conflicts are often a waste of time if the participants can't see eye to eye, and conflict management skills in the company might be lacking.

It's important to manage your emotions. Try not to overreact, as it will only make the situation worse. Think before you speak, as you can't take your words back once they are out there.

Clear communication is essential, as misunderstandings can also lead to conflict. When you send communication to your team, make sure they understand everything as you intended it to be understood.

Make sure your staff always understand exactly what you want from them. Don't criticize your employees unnecessarily, as they are entitled to their viewpoints. Be as calm and composed as possible.

If you have done something wrong, don't hesitate to admit your mistakes; instead, apologize. Apologizing can help prevent both conflict and tension.

Sometimes, to avoid conflict which could end up wasting a lot of your management time, it's best to keep people apart who don't get along.

For example, you may have two employees who are highly qualified and hard workers. They have both delivered successful projects for the company and have mentored junior staff members. However, as soon as they have to work together on a project, there is conflict between them. You have tried to resolve the issues by using various conflict management techniques, but with no success, as it made the issues between them worse.

You decide that the best option is to give them different key responsibility areas. You instruct them not to interfere in each other's work, and you make sure that they have as little to do with each other as possible. Some of your management colleagues question your techniques, but you tell them that you're only attempting to avoid a conflict that could lead to a lot of wasted time and energy.

If you see a conflict coming, ask yourself: If a fight breaks out, will it have any benefits or not? Don't encourage fights, as they could just lead to an increasingly negative environment in your team.

Basic Communication Skills to Prevent and Minimize Conflict

Effective basic communication skills can help your team prevent and minimize conflict.

The following skills are important:

- Team members all need to be good listeners and not jump to conclusions. Listen to the other side of a story as well.
- Have discussions with team members and don't listen to rumors. It's always better to discuss situations openly.
- Have an open forum where everyone can give input. Everyone must get the opportunity to express their views so that a middle way can be found.
- Patience is essential when it comes to avoiding conflicts, as you will always get people who want to provoke you to start fights. Don't be influenced by them and try, instead, to listen to your own instincts. Control your feelings and don't lose your temper, as this only makes situations worse.
- Be impartial to avoid and minimize conflicts. Support what is correct, even if it is your friends who have committed wrong. Keep everyone's input in mind; don't ignore people because you don't know them.
- Never criticize people and try to make them look less intelligent in front of other people. Rather, guide the person, and make them realize where they have gone wrong.
- Positive attitudes also go a long way in helping to prevent fights and conflicts in your work team. If there are mistakes, don't play the blame game and pass the blame around.

The Blame Game

It's important to understand why people blame each other, in order to minimize the potential for conflict. People who are anxious and fearful might try to avoid responsibility when things go wrong, as they may fear that people will see them in a bad light, or they could lose their jobs.

The blame game will waste a lot of your time and is unproductive. Conversations go in circles, as everyone tries to blame somebody else, and no one wants to take responsibility for their involvement in the situation or problem.

An example of an unproductive situation is where a project wasn't completed on time. Some staff members may point out that they were waiting for other members of the team to provide them with information. However, they never bothered to follow up before the deadline.

Others will deny any responsibility and claim they were waiting for others to tell them what needed to be done. Some team members might not get along with one of their colleagues, and then decide to make that person the scapegoat for the situation.

The blame game will make any conflict situation in the workplace much worse. It causes more frustration and will lead to a decline in productivity. Blaming others also takes the attention away from the problem.

The blame game can have a detrimental effect on your team's performance and morale. Team members may feel humiliated if they have been singled out for blame, especially if it's not their fault.

Individuals or teams may also end up being scapegoated while the real problem is elsewhere. The blame game can also lead to customers no longer trusting your business. If you're always saying another department is to blame and you can't help the customers with his inquiry it makes the whole organization seem incompetent.

The blame game can also lead to your organization becoming less innovative and creative. People won't try new things if they are scared they won't work, and this will reduce team performance in the long-term.

Types of People Who Like to Blame

Unfortunately, causing conflict and playing the blame game are part of some people's character. While you shouldn't let these types of people manipulate you or your other team members, treat them with understanding, as you don't know what has led to them becoming this way. However, don't initiate conflict with them.

- The 'victim' type may appear harmless at first, but their behavior can be toxic. They struggle to let go of the hurt they experienced in the past and they often blame other people for their inability to progress in life.

  The blame game just comes naturally to these people, and they have plenty of sad stories of their past life.

- Narcissists thrive on attention from the blame game. A narcissist is incapable of accepting responsibility, as they want everyone to believe they are superior. However, in reality, many of them are suffering from inferiority complexes.

- Pathological liars will lie about everything, and the blame game usually fits their agenda. They can be very creative in blaming other people for something which isn't their responsibility at all.

- People with low self-esteem also sometimes try to shift the blame. They sometimes try to pull others down with them.

- Arrogant or egotistical people will always go for the blame game. They tend to place the responsibility for their actions on everyone around them. In this way, one can keep on seeing themselves as a superior person. These are some of the most difficult people to get to face up to their responsibilities.

- Control freaks also tend to blame others. To admit failure to them would mean losing control of a situation.

You can't stop other people from playing the blame game. However, you can admit your own mistakes and model the correct behavior to your team. Here, empathy also plays an important role, as you need to be able to see things from other people's perspectives. As a manager, you also need to stop trying to control everything around you. You will never be able to fix or know everything, so it's best to loosen control. You can take responsibility for your own actions. As an adult, you should be able to own up to your mistakes. Rather use the energy that you usually use to deny your involvement to see how you can do things better in the future.

Knowing the Personalities of Your Team Members

Another way to minimize conflict in your workplace is to learn as much as you can about the personalities of your team members, in an effort to help everyone to get along better. Completing personality tests could even be a fun team-building activity for your team members to get to know each other better.

Benefits of Doing Personality Tests

Besides getting to know each other better, personality tests can also have all kinds of other useful benefits.

It can help you figure out where the strengths of your employees are, and in which areas they still need to improve. This is especially useful in a pressurized environment, as you can improve your productivity, by letting employees focus on areas where their strengths are. It also shows staff how they can be more productive.

It's also a good way to scan future potential employees to determine if they will fit in with the culture of your company.

There are several useful tests available that will help you get to know your team members better and understand their strengths and weaknesses.

Myers-Briggs Type Indicator (MTBI)

One of the most popular tests used by companies to do personality tests is the Myers-Briggs Type Indicator (MTBI) which is based on Carl Jung's theory of personality types. The test indicates 16 different personality types that are indicated as codes of four letters.

The MBTI test can give you a lot of insight into people's personalities. It's important to remember that the different personality types are all equally valuable.

The test can help you understand your own strengths, and those of others in your team at work. It's particularly useful when you're working on a project with a group because it can help you realize who is skilled at performing certain actions. It's easier to assign tasks, and the team can work together more successfully to achieve goals.

The MBTI should preferably be administered by a qualified practitioner and include a follow-up on the results.

Four Tendencies Framework

Another useful system for understanding people is American author Gretchen Rubin's Four Tendencies Framework. Rubin divides personalities into four categories, namely questioners, upholders, rebels and obligers, depending on how they respond to others' expectations. According to this theory, we respond to both outer expectations, such as work deadlines or requests, and inner expectations such as our desires to do something. The test can give us a deeper understanding of ourselves and others. You can complete the test on her website, at quiz.gretchenrubin.com/.

DiSC

The DiSC model was already designed in 1928 after the psychologist William Moulton Marston set out personality archetypes in his book *Emotions of Normal People*. The DiSC personality test measures attributes such as dominance, influence, steadiness and compliance. Most people will be dominant in one of these, and that is their superior personality attribute.

The test is available on 123Test.com.

Eysenck Personality Test

This personality test was developed by Hans Eysenck. He identified three elements that will affect a person's personality, namely extroversion, psychoticism, and neuroticism.

Studies have shown a link between psychoticism and creativity that can be useful in jobs that need a level of innovation. You can do the test at similarminds.com/eysenck.html.

Keirsey Temperament Sorter

This assessment was designed by Dr. David Keirsey and is based on his bestselling book, *Please Understand Me*. The aim of the assessment is to help professionals understand their temperament, character, and level of intelligence. You get to understand how your different personality characteristics impact your career, relationships, and team dynamics at work.

You can take this test at profile.keirsey.com/#/b2c/assessment/start.

Key Takeaways

- Conflict is inevitable when employees come from different backgrounds and have different views.

- The goal should be to resolve conflict in an efficient way.

- If conflict isn't resolved, it can become worse and affect productivity and morale in teams.

- The Thomas-Kilmann model was developed in the 1970s by the researchers Kenneth Thomas and Ralph Kilmann.

- The Kilmann model refers to 'conflict' as a condition in which people can't align their concerns with each other. If people care about contradictory things, you are bound to get into conflict.

- People who are fearful and anxious usually play the blame game, as they are too scared of the consequences to take responsibility.

- The blame game wastes valuable time in the office and is unproductive.

- Learning as much as you can about your employees' personalities is another way to minimize conflict. Completing personality tests could be a fun team building activity for team members to get to know each other better.

- Narcissistic people like playing the blame game.

Does Your Employee Suffer From a Mental Health Condition?

Mental illness can affect your employee's mood, thinking patterns, feelings, and behavior. As the person's manager, it can be difficult to know what to do, if you suspect your employee is suffering from a mental health condition, because you don't want to invade their privacy, but you also want to be supportive. However, you also need to be certain that they are not a danger to other employees or clients who may visit your company.

You can focus on the employee's behavior if it should come to a disciplinary situation, but you also need to know what could be signs of serious mental illness.

Mental health issues are also one of the most common reasons why employees could take time off from work. It could also affect the employee's productivity when they are at the office.

If you suspect it might be a serious problem, you might have to intervene.

The following could be signs that your employee has a serious mental health issue:

- Their appearance has become unhealthy and unkempt. People who suffer from mental health issues may have poor hygiene or they can suddenly start dressing inappropriately for work.
- The employee's behavior might become inconsistent and erratic. The person might start displaying mood swings and start behaving in strange and disturbing ways.
- The employee might also start to struggle to work with others and become easily irritated and frustrated. They might approach their work in a haphazard way.

- Eating and sleeping habits may also change if the person is struggling with a mental health problem. If a person never eats lunch anymore or starts to look like they haven't had a decent night's sleep in a long time, it could all be a warning sign of potential mental health issues.
- If the employee starts taking a lot of time off from work, it could also indicate a mental health issue.
- If the person is struggling to focus and has trouble solving problems, it could also be a sign of a mental health problem.
- The employee with mental health problems could also be paranoid about coworkers or even their employers. Their fears tend to be abnormal and they are usually anxious about keeping their job.
- The person might withdraw from social situations, especially with their coworkers. Some people isolate themselves, as they also tend to suffer from self-loathing.
- If the employee comes to work smelling of alcohol, or you suspect they might have taken drugs, they also likely have a mental health problem.

How Do You Manage an Employee Who Is Suffering From a Mental Health Crisis?

Make sure you are not acting impulsively or in a vacuum when you deal with a situation that is being caused by mental illness. Consult with your colleagues or other responsible employees and ask them if they have noticed the same behavior.

Also, consult with your Human Resources department. This is a complicated matter and you can't just deal with it like another performance issue, as the employee also has rights.

If you run a small business, you might need to get an outside consultant to advise you.

When you approach the employee, show them compassion. They might not be aware that they have a problem, or they don't want people to be aware of it. Offer them the opportunity to find help, if they are willing. You should inform yourself of what options are available through the company, and what help can be offered to the employee before you speak to them.

You will have to work together with the employee to reach a solution. Try to treat the person with kindness and respect and show them that you care about them as a person.

If your company has an employee assistance program, you can refer the troubled employee to this program. If the behavior that someone exhibits is unacceptable at work, you will have to document it. Mention to the employee that they will need to do something about that behavior, and recommend that they should make an appointment with a mental healthcare provider.

You can do this in different ways. It could be voluntary; just provide them with the resources they would need to give attention to their problem. If the problem is severe and the employee acknowledges they have a problem, but they refuse to get help, you can give them a final warning and a mandate that they must contact employee assistance, if your company has this option available.

You could also ask them to sign an agreement that they will find help, and their healthcare service provider must provide you with regular updates on their progress.

If the situation becomes intolerable and the employee is threatening you, you might realize that there is not much you can do to improve the situation. The last resort is that the employee might need to be removed from their position. This only happens after all other options have been exhausted.

Managing Employees Who Are Experiencing Stressful Life Experiences

You may also have to deal with employees who experience temporary stressful life situations that could influence their work attendance and the quality of their work or their work output. Even if your company has worked hard to create a psychologically safe work environment, people might not feel comfortable enough to tell you their marriage has fallen apart, or that one of their family members is extremely sick.

They may be embarrassed about the extent to which their work is being affected by their personal problems. It might be difficult for you at first to recognize that an employee is going through a difficult time, if they are good at covering up their emotions. That is also why you need to build trust with your employees and create a culture of sharing thoughts and emotions. If the culture in your office is compassionate, it is more likely that employees will come forward when they are going through a tough time.

This situation can also be difficult to handle for you as a manager, as you have to show empathy and care, but you should also not pry into the employee's personal business. You are not a psychologist, so it's best if you don't ask a lot of questions about the employee's problems.

If you ask too many questions, the employee might feel that they need to tell you more than they are comfortable with, since you are the person with power in the relationship. The idea is to build a caring relationship with employees, but not an overly friendly one. Don't confuse being liked with being respected.

When you speak to your employees about their current stressful situation, first listen to them, before you recommend a course of action to them.

Give them a chance to speak, as they might just want someone to listen to their difficulties about divorce, or caring for a sick relative, and how it has affected their attention span. Don't immediately tell them to take leave; first hear them out, as that is possibly not what they have been planning on doing.

Try asking them what the two of you can do about their performance during this difficult period. Ask how you can support them. They could possibly have ideas that could be acceptable to you, such as time off, or a more flexible schedule for a certain period.

Do research before you meet with the employee, on what the company can offer the employee under certain circumstances. You may want to offer employees the ability to take additional leave or the option to work from home, but if it doesn't work that way in your company, there is not much you can do about it. If you know outright what you can offer them, go ahead. Otherwise, tell them you will need to find out what is possible.

Check on the employee regularly to make sure they are doing as fine as they can be under the circumstances. The employee will appreciate that you care about them. Check regularly on how they are doing with the work, and ask them to let you know if they feel they are in over their heads.

Try to mitigate risks around the affected employee's workload early. It's essential to determine if the person's absence will affect other members in the team or your clients. If other people are willing to take on some of the person's projects, consider doing that temporarily. Just make sure you reward the people who will be doing the extra work.

Also, be sure to set timelines for the adjustments. If the employee knows the situation will last a few weeks, set a meeting date after that period to figure out what to do next. If it's a long-term situation, meet regularly to check with the employee, make adjustments to their work schedule, and discuss the expectations you have of them.

Just keep in mind that what you do now might set a precedent for future cases in which other employees experience problems. Other employees will take note of how you treat the struggling employee and will expect similar treatment if they experience difficult times.

If you want people to work productively, they will need to trust you and believe that you will treat them in a fair way at all times.

Set goals that are realistically possible for them to meet. The goals must be specific and based in reality.

Case Study: Offering Flexible Time

When Lucy, the owner of a content agency and communications consultancy heard that the wife of one of her best copywriters had been diagnosed with terminal cancer, she knew it was going to be a stressful and emotional time for him, especially since he also had to look after two children. It was difficult to say how much time his wife had left, as it seemed that the cancer wasn't spreading as fast as initially thought. However, his situation was extremely difficult and emotional, as the children were also struggling to cope with the situation. Lucy decided to decrease her employee's work burden. She offered him more flexible hours and the opportunity to work from home, which enabled him to spend more time looking after his wife, and he was also able to spend more time with his children. When his wife's health got so bad that he couldn't spend a lot of time on work, Lucy asked other writers to temporarily take over some of his projects. Two years after his wife passed away, the employee is still working at Lucy's company. Lucy allowed him to continue working on a flexible schedule part time from home, which helped him spend more time with his children and helped them adjust to their new situation.

General Office Stress

Unfortunately, many people today regard themselves as being successful, if they are stressed most of the time. Their health may be suffering, but they feel the need to be constantly busy, even if their work performance is in all likelihood declining from a lack of sleep and rest. Chronic stress is actually just bad for our health, and is nothing to be proud of. Our brains aren't equipped to be constantly under stress, and this could lead to overstimulation and medical conditions such as heart disease and hyperthyroidism.

Our offices can also overstimulate our brains with their harsh electrical lighting, noisy traffic outside, and the oversupply of caffeine we consume to get us through the day, especially if we haven't slept well the night before. Maybe it's time for us to start rushing around and slow down. The multitasking we are forced to do every day is also stressful, and it's not part of our biological nature to focus on multiple things at once.

The constant stress will cause your body to release more stress hormones which can also cause anxiety. Even sitting at a desk in the office for the entire day is stressful for your body, as you are meant to move around. That is why it's important to take frequent breaks, and mindfulness exercises can also help you relieve stress.

Key Takeaways

- Mental illness can affect your employee's mood, thinking patterns, feelings, and behavior. It can also affect the quality of their work and their overall productivity. It can be difficult to know what to do, if you suspect your employee is suffering from a mental health condition.

- You might have to intervene if you suspect the person could be suffering from a serious mental health disorder.

- Consult with your colleagues or other responsible employees and ask them if they have noticed changes in the employee's behavior. Make sure you are not working in a vacuum when you want to take action.

- You may also have to deal with employees who experience temporary stressful life situations that could influence the quality of their work and their productivity.

- Stress has become a badge of honor for many people, even though their health often suffers as a result of it.

- Our brains are overstimulated when we are constantly under stress, and this can lead to us developing other health conditions.

Chapter 5:

The Steps to a Psychologically Safe Organization

The idea of having to make big changes in your organization in order to move toward a psychologically safe environment might seem overwhelming at first. However, one of the best places to start can be to take a validated EQ test to determine your own emotional intelligence. Before you can make changes to your organization, you first need to know your own EQ results.

Complete a Validated EQ Test

The best place to start when you want to promote a culture of emotional intelligence in your business is to get those in leadership positions to complete validated EQ tests. <u>The EQ test from 6 seconds</u> is a good option.

When managers know their EQ results, it will be easier to know where you should start your journey.

The Solution

Managers: Focus on Your Own Emotional Intelligence First

Before you can encourage emotional intelligence and health among your employees, you need to start with yourself.

Are you an emotionally healthy person? Are you able to deal with the daily stress without overreacting to challenges at work?

Attributes of an Emotionally Healthy Person

If you're emotionally healthy, you're aware of your feelings and able to manage them. You're also able to cope well during difficult times and treat everyone around you with compassion and empathy.

Emotionally healthy people also practice self-care and look after their bodies. You'll be able to handle stress well and remain calm during times of chaos.

For example, you're the type of person that is able to keep up in a dynamic, fast-paced environment. You manage to persevere through times of high stress, but take care of your own needs as well. You also accept that jobs will sometimes go wrong and that errors will be made. The constant pressure could have made you irritable with your employees, and you could have started to rely on unhealthy coping mechanisms like alcohol and drugs, but you manage to be your best self every day.

Improving Your Emotional Health Through Mindfulness

Emotional health is about living a balanced life and being resilient when you get knocked down. There will always be problems and stress in life, and you will need to be able to thrive despite this.

Working on your emotional health can be difficult, as it involves giving attention to your behavior, feelings, and thoughts. First of all, you need to understand what your emotions mean to you.

You can improve your emotional health by practicing mindfulness.

When you practice mindfulness, you need to be aware of your emotions and surroundings. You need to consciously focus your attention on what you're hearing, seeing, and feeling in the present moment. The idea is to ignore the thoughts that are racing through your head and only focus on what is happening now.

Practicing mindfulness can help you make better decisions. When you're mindful, you accept your emotions and thoughts. You'll also be able to react to others in a healthy way.

People who aren't mindful also tend to play the blame game and struggle to accept responsibility for their faults. They usually struggle to control their emotions and their thoughts, which tend to run on autopilot.

Mindfulness can help you strengthen your mental health in the following ways:

- It will be easier for you to process stress in a healthy way. If you're not able to process stress, you could end up developing depression or anxiety.
- Mindfulness can also help you manage your emotions, which is especially useful if you work in a stressful environment, as it

will help you act calmly instead of having emotional outbursts when you experience problems at work.

- Mindfulness is also great for your physical health, as it can improve your sleep, reduce your appetite, and boost your mood. It can also help lessen pain.

Practicing Mindfulness

There are mindfulness techniques you can use to quiet your mind and anchor you in the present.

5-5-5 Breathing Technique

You can do this exercise while you're sitting down or even while you're standing or lying down.

Breathe in for five seconds, hold your breath for another five seconds, and then breathe out for five seconds.

Pay attention to everything you feel when you breathe in through your nose, fill your lungs, and then breathe out again. This exercise will also help you with anxiety and stress.

You can also do mindfulness exercises while going for a walk. This is a good way of relaxing your mind while getting exercise at the same time. The exercise will take you 10 to 15 minutes. You can do it on its own, or as part of your fitness routine.

Walk at a natural pace and count your steps from one to ten to help you concentrate.

Experience the process of walking and lifting your feet and putting them down again. How does it feel when you put your feet down on the ground?

Take note of your surroundings, but continue to focus on walking.

While you are doing this exercise, you can also perform the 5-5-5 breathing meditation.

Office Mindfulness

You can do this body awareness exercise at work if you have your own office. This exercise can also help you focus on your body and help you reduce your anxiety. It can even help you settle your breathing and heart rate.

You can do this exercise lying down or sitting in a comfortable chair. If you are lying down, put your arms by your side with your palms up.

Stay as still and calm as possible. If you do need to move around, do it mindfully while being aware of all the sensations.

Consider how you're breathing. Your breathing should be low and steady. Also, notice the rhythm and feel yourself inhaling and exhaling.

Take note of sensations such as your breathing, heartbeat, the texture of your clothes, and your muscles. Experience sensations through your entire body, from your feet to your head, while concentrating on each part.

When you've completed the exercise, open your eyes slowly while adjusting to your surroundings.

Mindfulness and Emotional Hygiene

Mindfulness can also help you shut out the sensory and mental information that bombards you every day. If you want to stop yourself from overthinking, focus on your breathing, as it will stop your thoughts from spiraling out of control.

You can focus your attention through mindfulness techniques. Another good way of practicing mindfulness and improving your emotional well-being is by practicing gratitude on a daily basis. You can also do this by journaling.

Make lists of what you are grateful for every day. Include people in your life, belongings, and experiences. Also, write down reasons why you are grateful.

This can give you a new perspective and help you to be grateful for the good things you have in your life. Try to remove selfish emotions and thoughts from your mind. Feel kindness and love for yourself, and also for other people.

Emotional hygiene is also important when it comes to improving your emotional intelligence. How do you clean your mind? It's not as easy as cleaning your body, but positive thinking will help.

It can be difficult to change a negative thought pattern once you are used to thinking like this.

Do you find it difficult to stop thinking about negative events that happened in the past? Take care that you don't get stuck in a spiral of rumination that could lead to anxiety or depression. If you are the type of person who has this problem, it's a good idea to try and distract yourself to break the cycle.

Buy some paint and put down your feelings in bright colors on paper. This creative activity should free you from your oppressive thoughts and give you an outlet from your downward spiral of negativity.

If you're stressed and feel as if you're in emotional pain, don't ignore this, or tell yourself that you'll deal with it later. It will become worse, and you will find it much harder to deal with at a later stage.

Be gentle with yourself. While you shouldn't blame others when things go wrong, you also shouldn't blame yourself for every little mistake or tell yourself that you deserve to fail. Believe that you're good enough, and that you're working hard enough to reach your goals. You need healthy self-esteem, as this will strengthen your emotional resilience.

If you've had a hard day and you feel that you're emotions are out of control, do the following:

- Relax as much as possible. Do breathing exercises if you can.
- Don't compare your achievements and failures to those of other people.
- If one of your projects failed, force yourself to accept that everything can't be your fault. There are many factors that could have played a role, as well as many other people who were involved.
- Try to see the negative situation as a learning experience.
- Keep a positive outlook with the future in mind. While things are bad today, they might be better tomorrow.
- Also, assess the situation and exactly what went wrong. See what you can do to prevent the same situation from happening again in future.

Key Takeaways

- Managers need to start the journey to creating a psychologically safe environment for employees by improving their own emotional intelligence.

- Practicing mindfulness can help you make better decisions, and you will also be able to form healthier relationships.

- There are mindfulness techniques you can use to quiet your mind and anchor yourself in the present, like the 5-5-5 breathing technique.

A Plan to Increase the EQ in Your Organization

Look back at the strategies from Chapter 3 and focus on increasing the EQ of your employees and organization. Keep following these steps, combined with your own research and training, until you experience personal growth or experience positive changes in the organization, or in the relationships with your employees.

Select some of the other strategies if you feel your team needs to do more work.

Choose one to two strategies from Chapter 4 to improve the EQ and psychological safety of your organization.

Presenteeism and emotional detachment at work should be part of your plan to improve the EQ in your company.

Presenteeism and Emotional Detachment at Work

Presenteeism is also popularly known as "butt-in-seat time." This refers to managers who judge their employees and teams based on how many hours they have been at work, in front of their PC, rather than by the end product and contributions they deliver. If you have managers and employees in your company with this mentality, you have a lot of work ahead of you.

What Is the Cause?

Presenteeism also takes place when employees come to work sick, or they may have other problems, which means they are not really focusing on what they are doing. If people are distracted at work as a result of personal problems or chronic illness, you will experience a drop in employee performance.

Presenteeism can also be the result of internal or external pressure. If you have a manager who sets unrealistic deadlines, employees might work while they are supposed to be on holiday, and not focus on what they're doing. As well, they may try to work while they're sick and distracted.

Employees are entitled to some form of paid time off, be this vacation, sick days, or holidays. However, the problem creeps in when you have managers who persuade their employees that they shouldn't take time off, even when they are ill. This is related to the idea that if you are loyal to your job and company, you need to be present at work at all times.

However, workplaces that function like this will often have poorly motivated staff and their productivity will also be low. Staff tend to become resentful and unmotivated. Companies in which employees are respected and told to take their time off for a better work-life balance, will have more energetic workers.

It may seem that it's better for the business bottom line if employees work more, but that is actually not the case. People who work when they're ill can infect other people, and this can be deadly to immunocompromised workers, especially if you have a disease like COVID-19. The truth is that presenteeism actually ends up costing businesses a lot of money.

Fixing Presenteeism

Presenteeism can be fixed and won't happen in companies that have a psychologically safe culture.

Presenteeism is a workplace culture problem, and fixing it should start with the top management of the company. Senior management needs to manage the desired behavior of staff by staying at home when they are ill or unable to focus on work. If the leadership of the company doesn't use their sick leave, hard workers who want to climb the corporate ladder won't use them either.

Supplying enough sick leave is vital. Employees won't be able to stay home and recover if they don't have paid leave. Managers also need to encourage employees to take their vacation time. A psychologically safe organization has a culture that recognizes employees have lives and they need time off from work.

Another way to address presenteeism is to make employees feel that their jobs really matter. Some employees may start to feel invisible and as if their jobs don't really matter.

Emotional Detachment

Emotional detachment can also be regarded as a form of presenteeism. The problems of people who are emotionally detached could be of a personal nature or could be caused by their workplace situation.

Someone who is emotionally detached will also keep to themself and won't be willing to connect to anyone on an emotional level. This employee could be using this detachment as a coping mechanism to deal with stressful situations, especially in very busy offices. Some employees could also choose to detach themselves if they find themselves working in a toxic office with a lot of drama between employees. If you find that there is tension among colleagues, you need to use the conflict management techniques discussed earlier to get to the bottom of the situation and sort it out.

Employees who are emotionally detached at work might display the following symptoms:

- They never share emotions or feelings and they're unwilling to participate in team initiatives that try to encourage positive interaction between colleagues.

- They usually appear preoccupied around people, and not really interested in what others are doing or saying. They also seem to find it difficult to empathize with other people's emotions.
- Also note that if people behave like this, it could be a symptom of a mental health condition.

How can you, as a manager, deal with emotional detachment? What are other red flags for emotional detachment? How do you know if and when you should address the issue? When a staff member is quiet during a meeting, one might just think they have nothing to say, but it can be worrying if this becomes a pattern for someone who usually has a lot to say at meetings. It could suggest that they really want to be somewhere else.

When a once responsive employee stops replying to emails or taking part in work-related discussions, it should also be a red flag. Reach out to them and try to determine if there is a problem. It could be nothing serious, but it's worth getting to the root of it.

If an employee is regularly absent from work, it might be time to sit down with them and talk about the situation. If you notice an increasingly cranky and negative attitude, it's also a good idea to have a talk with the employees, as it could be that they are just overworked.

Another sign of increasing detachment is if someone's quality of work goes down, especially if the employee was known to have high standards and be vigilant.

There are many reasons why an employee may have become detached from a job, ranging from personal problems to burnout. It's important to start a conversation with them to determine the cause of the situation and what can be done to motivate them again. You need to be patient and empathetic, as you can never be sure what is happening in the personal lives of your employees.

Building Resilience and a Psychologically Safe Work Environment

If you are resilient, you will have the ability to adapt to difficult circumstances or events. Resilient people can respond successfully to environmental challenges and they are also resistant to the effects of stress.

People who aren't resilient tend to dwell on their problems and turn to unhealthy coping mechanisms, such as drugs and alcohol.

Resilient people still face challenges, but have a better ability to deal with them, as well as stress in general. Resilient people also have a stronger ability to keep on functioning through adversity. One of the key elements of being resilient is also being able to reach out to other people for support.

Resilient leaders can also help employees to deal better with changes and help them be less susceptible to burnout. They can also help employees improve their overall well-being, including their mental and physical health.

Managers can help their teams become resilient and will also contribute to the psychological safety of the company.

Leaders and employees who are able to focus on the positive during challenging times are usually more resilient. This positive attitude also contributes to creating a psychologically safe work environment.

Resilient people who are calm, optimistic, and confident create the best work environments wherein employees can share their success and appreciate each other's contributions to the team.

Psychological safety also makes employees more resilient at work, if people don't have to constantly fear the consequences of what they say and do at work. This will make them more able to process critical information, and understand their past mistakes. This will give your team a strategic advantage, as the combination of psychological safety and resilience prepares the employees for future challenges.

Before you set out to improve the psychological safety and resilience of your workplace, you need to measure the current psychological safety of your team. The easiest option would be to let them complete an assessment, with questions asking them about how they are treated, if they make mistakes, and if they think it is safe to take risks while they are working on this team.

An assessment won't necessarily prove that your workplace is safe, but it can help you identify strengths and areas that still need improvement.

You can do the assessment with a survey tool like SurveyMonkey. One example would be to ask employees to rate certain statements on a scale of 1-5. You can rate them from 1 being strongly disagree, to 5 being strongly agree.

Ask them questions, such as if they feel safe taking risks at the organization, or if people are rejected at the organization for being different.

An organizational survey can also be done to get an idea of the cultural issues in the company that could be impacting psychological safety.

Once you understand how your team ranks when it comes to psychological safety, you can focus on interventions to improve.

Approach to Improving Psychological Safety

Workshops or coaching are just some of the interventions you can implement.

There needs to be clarity about the organization's values. Management needs to communicate the organization's mission, vision, and values through all the layers of the organization and managers, on the different levels needed to work together to understand and evaluate them. They also need to be improved where needed. Management must also live the values and model them to the rest of the staff.

Management needs to be provided with training in psychological safety, emotional intelligence, and leadership to create teams that perform well.

Provide your team with the tools that will help them be successful. They need ways to offer feedback, report incidents, and identify their concerns.

The company needs to develop an approach to resolve challenges and learn from errors, rather than blaming staff for them. Look at ways to move on, and how processes can be changed to prevent future errors.

Promote an atmosphere of understanding and cooperation. Listen to your team members when they come to you with feedback, or their problems and ideas. If you show that you're interested in listening to them, it will make them more engaged with their work.

You also need to learn your team members' preferred communication style at work and then deal with them in this way.

Lifelong Learning

Psychological safety in the workplace also supports a culture of lifelong learning, which is becoming increasingly important in the constantly changing knowledge economy.

If you want to grow your organization, your employees must grow and increase their knowledge and skills as well. The need to continue learning is greater than ever with the changing needs of the knowledge economy. Employees are under constant pressure to learn as the relevant shelf life of their skills decreases.

One of the greatest benefits of psychological safety in an organization is that it creates an environment where people are willing to learn on a continuous basis. Employees are much more likely to adapt and learn in an environment where learning from mistakes is celebrated instead of punished.

Otherwise, there is the risk that employees will become anxious about learning, and become defensive when they make mistakes and things don't go well.

Fear is a barrier to learning, and people will perform poorly when their brain is flooded with fight-or-flight chemicals. Fear takes resources away from parts of the brain that manage your working memory and processes new information. Fear also impairs analytical thinking and problem-solving, and as a result, people tend to be less innovative and creative.

It will be difficult to transform your organization into a learning organization if mistakes are regarded as embarrassing rather than opportunities to improve and learn.

Leaders who don't grow get stuck in a rut. They can't grow and change their teams, and they won't be able to make a meaningful contribution to the organization.

Organizations may also need to put in more work to encourage employees to keep on learning. Many employees will only improve their skills if it's part of their job requirement. There are also those employees who will always keep on resisting continuous learning.

Encourage Learning

Learning together as a team can inspire your team to aim for higher performance. It can also help your team to build confidence and motivation.

In addition, you can try the following practices to encourage learning behavior and psychological safety:

We have said this before, but learn to embrace mistakes. How your team deals with successes and failures will also determine if people feel safe learning. Teams also need to realize that projects or ideas fail, but not people. Make it safe for your employees to ask questions about what worked and what didn't.

Focus on growing the people on your team, and discuss their envisaged career paths with them. Encourage a culture of knowledge sharing in your team, where your employees can share their work and non-work expertise. Also, share your knowledge with them.

Make it easy for your employees to learn. Your employees will learn more if it is made easier for them, and if it's part of their daily activities at work. If employees have access to online learning, it's also easier for them to learn wherever they want and when they have the time. Keep your employees informed of training and learning opportunities. Make sure that the training is available to everyone and not only those who have been identified as having high potential.

Personal development should be led by employees and not managers. Encourage your employees to discover what they are interested in, and what they want to learn. Make sure they know enough to make their own career and learning choices. Get your employees to think about the skills they want.

Employees are also more likely to keep on learning if their manager is a lifelong learner. Also encourage them to read books, talk with people in your industry, and attend conferences.

Lifelong Learning and Continuous Learning

When it comes to creating a learning environment, one also needs to understand the difference between a continuous and lifelong learning environment.

Lifelong learning usually refers to individuals who make a long-term commitment to learning new skills and gaining knowledge.

The lifelong learner will also usually incorporate continuous learning as part of their lifestyle. This type of learner is usually also focused on long-term improvement and will often have a schedule for learning new things, such as reading about something new for a specific time period every day.

The continuous learner is also committed to learning new skills, but in a formal or temporary context. An example of a formal commitment is someone who is learning new skills for their job.

You can build a continuous learning environment in your company by encouraging your employees to take part in continuous learning. Some employees will take part and will be motivated, but many will not have the time or the resources to do it. Employees who are focused on the job might also be scared that learning will be seen as a waste of time.

A way to encourage reluctant employees to learn is to create a learning plan. Employees are more likely to become involved if continuous learning becomes part of the way the business operates.

The plan can include the different types of learning and support that employees may need, such as mobile learning, and mentoring if it's available.

Other resources that can help with continuous learning can include:

- A personal development plan that you need to complete for each employee to determine what they want to learn.
- Setting time aside for employees to engage in learning or training.
- Organizing mentorship and coaching.
- Setting aside opportunities to attend events and team workshops.
- Providing professional resources via memberships to organizations or subscriptions.

- Giving access to online learning via self-paced courses.

Benefits of Continuous Learning

A learning culture will not only improve innovation and the performance culture of your organization, but also employee satisfaction. It will also have the following benefits for your company:

- Employees will be empowered, and they will be able to contribute more on a higher level to the company.
- It will cost the company less money to train and upskill existing employees than to hire and train new ones.
- If you nominate your employees for continuous learning, it also shows them that you consider them to be a worthwhile investment for the company, and that you are serious about wanting to develop employees.

Key Takeaways

- Presenteeism also takes place when employees come to work sick, or they may have other problems, which means they are not really focusing on what they are doing.

- Presenteeism is also the result of managers who persuade their employees that they shouldn't take time off, even when they are ill. This is related to the idea that if you are loyal to your job and company, you need to be present at work at all times.

- Presenteeism won't happen in companies with a psychologically safe culture. Fixing this problem should start with the top management of the company.

- When a once responsive employee stops replying to emails or taking part in work-related discussions, it could indicate that there is a problem, and you should reach out to them.

- Resilient people can bounce back from difficult circumstances or events.

- Psychological safety in the workplace also supports a culture of lifelong learning. It's becoming increasingly important that employees should keep on learning in the changing knowledge economy.

Conclusion

This book has considered the responsibility of management to create a psychologically safe work environment to the benefit of all employees, along with continued profitability of their organization. However, before cultural change can be effected in their organizations, managers first need to focus on learning as much as they can about emotional intelligence, and establishing and improving their own emotional intelligence. To be able to do this, you need to be an emotionally healthy person and able to deal with life's challenges, as well as the daily stress that will come your way.

How to Make This Book Work for You

This book gives you important insight into emotional intelligence and how emotionally intelligent leaders operate. If you didn't have an understanding of emotional intelligence, you should now be able to grasp all the basic concepts of it, and also understand how to improve your emotional intelligence as well as that of your employees. You should now also understand the role emotional intelligence plays in the creation of a psychologically safe organization.

Emotionally intelligent managers can manage their emotions in a way that allows them to achieve their goals. They can maintain a positive climate in the office, and they're able to change the culture of their teams for the better. This is the type of manager you should aim to become.

A mutual relationship based on trust and respect is central to this. If you and your employees don't trust and respect each other, you will have to work hard to get there, before you can truly create an atmosphere of psychological safety. Remember that you need to treat your employees like the professional adults they are, and sometimes this will mean taking a step back, and not being a micromanager. They were hired for their skills and what they can bring to the company, so there is no reason that you should be managing every little thing they do. This just creates a situation of mistrust, and respect will be lost on both sides.

Finally, it's also about showing your employees that you really care for them. The best managers always treat their employees like valuable humans, and not like machines that don't have feelings and have to keep on producing without taking breaks.

Chapter Takeaways

The chapters of this book all offer unique insights on emotional intelligence and psychological safety.

Chapter 1

Chapter 1 gives you a background on emotional intelligence. This is especially helpful if you have never been exposed to these concepts before, and now have to learn as fast as possible.

The chapter considers who need emotional intelligence to thrive in their businesses and careers, and when work environments can be considered to be psychologically safe.

The five components of emotional intelligence—self-awareness, self-management, social awareness, empathy, and motivation—are discussed in more detail.

Chapter 2

Chapter 2 considers why emotional intelligence is vital for organizations. It's also discussed as being an essential requirement for a good manager. The connection of higher emotional intelligence and high job satisfaction is discussed.

Chapter 3

This chapter considers the emotional foundations we would have built in childhood, and how that still influences our behavior as adults. If you have childhood trauma, understanding your childhood emotions will help you understand yourself better as an adult.

Eustress and distress are discussed, as well as the differences between these two types of stress.

The chapter also discusses how managers become victims of burnout, and how this can be prevented. It's essential that you also prioritize your own mental health and delegate work to your employees, which is also an opportunity for them to increase their skills and knowledge.

Mindfulness can help managers and employees manage their emotions and stay focused in the moment. If you want to be a mindful manager, you need to let go of your idea that there is only one acceptable way of doing things. Mindfulness exercises can help you start your day with the right mindset.

This chapter also looks at building trust and respect in our relationships at work. These are the core building blocks for creating psychological safety in the workplace.

Managers and employees need to get to know each other in order to build trust. Show employees you appreciate them, even in small ways, and they are much more likely to go the extra mile for the company.

The importance of respectful and clear feedback is also highlighted.

Chapter 4

Chapter 4 looks at corporate culture and how to create a passionate workforce. An open-door policy and one-on-one meetings can help you get to the bottom of issues before they get worse. These initiatives can also assist you in your goal to build healthy relationships, based on trust and respect.

Conflict management can be challenging. Conflict is inevitable if you have employees working together who are from different backgrounds. Effective conflict resolution is discussed, as well as how to avoid the blame game.

The chapter also provides advice on how to intervene if you suspect your employee is going through a stressful time at home, or might even be suffering from a mental health condition.

Chapter 5

Chapter 5 asks you to consider the different solutions that were provided throughout the book. It takes a more in-depth look at improving your emotional intelligence, and how mindfulness can help you on your journey. Problems like presenteeism in the workplace and emotional detachments are also discussed. Resilience and lifelong learning are also building blocks of creating a psychological safe work environment.

Final Thoughts

I trust that this book will help you take your first steps on your journey to creating a psychologically safe and emotionally intelligent workplace. A psychologically safe workplace is the office of the future, where all employees can contribute optimally without the fear of retributions.

I would appreciate it if you could leave a written review of this book, instead of a product rating. I am looking forward to receiving your input.

References

Alice Miller - *Child Abuse and Mistreatment.* (2015, September 11). http://www.alice-miller.com/en/

Alton, L. (n.d.). *How To Individualize Your Modern Workforce For Greater Employee Retention.* Forbes. Retrieved June 3, 2022, from https://www.forbes.com/sites/larryalton/2016/07/12/how-to-individualize-your-modern-workforce-for-greater-employee-retention/?sh=4d4acf36185f

Angus Ridgway. (2018, October 9). *People management: how to create a psychologically safe environment at work.* HRZone. https://www.hrzone.com/lead/culture/people-management-how-to-create-a-psychologically-safe-environment-at-work

Atlassian. (n.d.). *How to create a culture of knowledge sharing | Team Central.* Atlassian. https://www.atlassian.com/work-management/knowledge-sharing/culture

Blogger, G. (n.d.). *Individualize Your Employee Engagement Approach.* Www.bamboohr.com. Retrieved June 3, 2022, from https://www.bamboohr.com/blog/optimize-employee-engagement/

Cherry, K. (2021, July 23). *An Overview of the Myers-Briggs Type Indicator.* Verywell Mind; Verywellmind. https://www.verywellmind.com/the-myers-briggs-type-indicator-2795583

Çekmecelioğlu, Hülya & Günsel, Ayşe & Ulutaş, Tuğçe. (2012). *Effects Of Emotional Intelligence On Job Satisfaction: An Empirical Study On Call Center Employees.* Procedia - Social and Behavioral Sciences. 58. 363–369. 10.1016/j.sbspro.2012.09.1012.

Conflict at Workplace - Why Conflict Should be Avoided ? (2015). Managementstudyguide.com. https://www.managementstudyguide.com/conflict-at-workplace.htm

Council, F. C. (n.d.). *Council Post: How The Most Effective Managers Give Feedback.* Forbes. Retrieved June 3, 2022, from https://www.forbes.com/sites/forbescoachescouncil/2016/10/21/how-the-most-effective-managers-give-feedback/?sh=338bd5a6546b

Creating a Culture of Knowledge Sharing: Improving your Productivity and your Bottom Line | CCC Blog. (2018, August 14). Copyright Clearance Center. https://www.copyright.com/blog/culture-of-knowledge-sharing-improving-productivity-bottom-line/

Dealing With Conflicts: The Thomas-Kilmann Way. (2020, September 11). Harappa. https://harappa.education/harappa-diaries/thomas-kilmann-model-for-dealing-with-conflicts/#:~:text=In%20the%201970s%2C%20researchers%20Kenneth%20Thomas%20and%20Ralph,each%20other%2C%20then%20the%20outcome%20is%20conflict.%20

The Differences Between Eustress and Distress. (2021, December 23). Exploring Your Mind. https://exploringyourmind.com/the-differences-between-eustress-and-distress

Effective leaders have a high degree of EQ - emotional intelligence. (n.d.). Www.linkedin.com. https://www.linkedin.com/pulse/most-effective-leaders-have-high-degree-emotional-eq-dave-l-preece/?articleId=6094857217851351040

4 Reasons why social intelligence matters at work. (2018). Skills Portal. https://www.skillsportal.co.za/content/4-reasons-why-social-intelligence-matters-work

14 Ways To Build Trust in the Workplace. (n.d.). Indeed Career Guide. https://www.indeed.com/career-advice/career-development/building-trust

How Employees Can Give Feedback to Their Boss. (n.d.). Lattice.com. https://lattice.com/library/how-employees-can-give-feedback-to-their-boss

How should you use personality tests in the workplace? (2021, June 20). TestGorilla. https://www.testgorilla.com/blog/personality-tests-workplace/

How to Build Trust: In a Team, Workplace or With Your Employees. (n.d.). Tonyrobbins.com. https://www.tonyrobbins.com/business/building-trust-in-workplace/

How to Create Psychological Safety and Resilience in the Workplace | Black Diamond Leadership. (2021, February 22). https://www.blackdiamondleadership.com/psychological-safety-and-resilience/

How to measure psychological safety at your company. (2019, October 2). The Predictive Index. https://www.predictiveindex.com/blog/how-to-measure-psychological-safety/

Inc.Africa. (n.d.). Incafrica.com. Retrieved June 3, 2022, from https://incafrica.com/library/indigo-triplett-steps-you-can-take-to-manage-an-employee-demonstrating-mental-illness

IQ vs EQ: Emotional Intelligence in the Workplace. (2016, September 14). CU Online. https://online.campbellsville.edu/business/iq-vs-eq/

Is EQ more important in the Future of Work? - HR Future. (2017, August 24). Www.hrfuture.net. https://www.hrfuture.net/future-of-work/digital-economy/is-eq-more-important-in-the-future-of-work/

Kashyap, S. (2016, December 12). *How important it is to be socially aware at work?* Medium. https://kashyapsandeep.medium.com/how-important-it-is-to-be-socially-aware-at-work-a524cccba5c5

Lavoie, A. (n.d.). *Letting Your Employees Review You Can Lead to Personal and Professional Growth.* Entrepreneur. Retrieved June 3, 2022, from https://www.entrepreneur.com/article/239778

Link, G., Facebook, Twitter, Pinterest, Email, & Apps, O. (n.d.). *The Importance Of Motivating Your Team Psychologically Safely And Successfully.* Retrieved June 3, 2022, from https://www.polishedbytime.com/2021/11/the-importance-of-motivating-your-team.html

The link between Resilience and Psychological Safety: How resilient individuals create a psychologically safe environment…. (n.d.). Www.linkedin.com. Retrieved June 3, 2022, from https://www.linkedin.com/pulse/link-between-resilience-psychological-safety-how-resilient-cooper/

Managing Conflicts in the Workplace: An Introduction. (n.d.). Www.indeed.com. https://www.indeed.com/hire/c/info/managing-conflicts-in-the-workplace

Miao, C., Humphrey, R.H. and Qian, S. (2017), A meta-analysis of emotional intelligence and work attitudes. J Occup Organ Psychol, 90: 177-202. https://doi.org/10.1111/joop.12167

Mindfulness for Leaders: Improving Management Practices. (2018, February 8). LiquidPlanner. https://www.liquidplanner.com/blog/mindfulness-for-leaders-improving-management-practices/

Mishra, A., & Sengupta, S. (2021, May 12). *Thomas Kilmann Conflict Model.* Management Weekly. https://managementweekly.org/thomas-kilmann-conflict-resolution-model/

MyHub, T. (2018, June 28). *Mindfulness In The Workplace: Practical Ways To Introduce It.* MyHub Intranet Solutions. https://www.myhubintranet.com/mindfulness-in-the-workplace/

O'Hara, C. (2018, July 9). *How to Manage an Employee Who's Having a Personal Crisis*. Harvard Business Review. https://hbr.org/2018/07/how-to-manage-an-employee-whos-having-a-personal-crisis

Open Door Policy: What is, Meaning & Importance at Workplace. (2021, October 5). HIGH5 TEST. https://high5test.com/open-door-policy/

Panel®, E. (n.d.). *Council Post: 14 Leaders Share Their Insights On The Importance Of EQ*. Forbes. Retrieved June 3, 2022, from https://www.forbes.com/sites/forbesbusinesscouncil/2020/08/31/14-leaders-share-their-insights-on-the-importance-of-eq/?sh=a9a6b9d3e4fb

Patel, N. (2017, October 10). *10 ways to build resilience in your employees*. Resilience Counselling Network. https://www.resiliencecounsellingnetwork.com/10-ways-to-build-resilience-in-your-employees/

Presenteeism (and How Much It Costs Employers). (2019, June 25). The Balance Careers. https://www.thebalancecareers.com/what-is-presenteeism-what-does-it-cost-employers-4571002

Psychological safety and learning behavior in work teams. (n.d.). Www.marie-Claireross.com. Retrieved June 3, 2022, from https://www.marie-claireross.com/blog/psychological-safety-and-learnin-behaviour-in-work-teams

Resilient Leaders Create an Environment of Psychological Safety. (n.d.). Www.linkedin.com. Retrieved June 3, 2022, from https://www.linkedin.com/pulse/resilient-leaders-create-environment-psychological-potter-cpsychol/

Resources, H. (2020, December 1). *How managers can give better feedback.* Yespartners2017. https://yespartners.com/how-managers-can-give-better-feedback/

Shafir, H. (2020, November 6). *Eustress vs Distress: Positive & Negative Types of Stress.* Choosing Therapy. https://www.choosingtherapy.com/eustress-vs-distress/

Should Employees Review Their Bosses? (2014, November 18). HuffPost. https://www.huffpost.com/entry/should-employees-review-t_b_6180826

Stop Playing the "Blame Game": Finding Solutions Rather than Finding Fault. (n.d.). Www.mindtools.com. https://www.mindtools.com/pages/article/newCDV_56.htm

10 Best Workplace Personality Tests for Effective Teams - WorkStyle. (n.d.). Www.workstyle.io. Retrieved June 3, 2022, from https://www.workstyle.io/workplace-personality-test#:~:text=%2010%20Most%20Popular%20Workplace%20Personality%20Tests%20

10 Mindfulness Exercises for Work and Purpose. (2019, October 5). Mindfulness Exercises. https://mindfulnessexercises.com/10-mindfulness-exercises-for-work-and-purpose/#:~:text=%20Mindfulness%20Exercises%20at%20the%20Workplace%20%201

10 Warnings Signs Your Employee Has a Mental Health Issue. (2019, December 5). Discovery Mood & Anxiety Program. https://discoverymood.com/blog/warnings-signs-your-employee-has-a-mental-health-issue/

Theophilus Tagoe & Emmanuel Nii-Boye Quarshie (2016). *The relationship between emotional intelligence and job satisfaction among nurses in Accra.* DOI: 10.1002

TOP 10 Tips for Conflict Management Techniques Skills. (2016, February 29). EDUCBA. https://www.educba.com/conflict-management-techniques/

12 Mindfulness Exercises ideal for busy employees at work | Symonds Training. (2020, February 9). Symonds Research Training Course Materials. https://symondsresearch.com/mindfulness-exercises-employees/

Valamis. (2019). *Valamis.* Valamis. https://www.valamis.com/hub/lifelong-learning

Watson, E. T. (2021, July 8). *How does social awareness help you with your work life balance?* Medium. https://elissatealwatson.medium.com/how-does-social-awareness-help-you-with-your-work-life-balance-155cbc335dc0

What Does Having an Open Door Policy at Work Mean for Employees? The Balance Careers. https://www.thebalancecareers.com/open-door-policy-1918203

What is Presenteeism at Work and How to Handle it? (2021, December 9). Chanty. https://www.chanty.com/blog/presenteeism-at-work/

Yamada, D. (2010, August 2). *Is emotional detachment an antidote for a nasty workplace?* Minding the Workplace. https://newworkplace.wordpress.com/2010/08/02/is-emotional-detachment-an-antidote-for-a-nasty-workplace/#:~:text=Emotional%20detachment%20may%20be%20related%20to%20the%20concept